Advanced Theoretical Neural Networks with Python

Jamie Flux

https://www.linkedin.com/company/golden-dawn-engineering/

Contents

2

Chapter 1

Theoretical Frameworks of Neural Networks

Statistical Learning Theory

Statistical learning theory provides the foundation for understanding the performance of learning algorithms. Central to this framework are the concepts of risk minimization and overfitting. The goal of a learning algorithm is to approximate a function $f\colon \mathcal{X} \to \mathcal{Y}$ by a hypothesis h from a hypothesis space $\mathcal{H}$. The expected risk or generalization error is defined as:

$$R(h) = \int_{\mathcal{X} \times \mathcal{Y}} L(h(x), y) \, dP(x, y)$$

where L is a loss function and $P(x, y)$ is the joint distribution over input-output pairs. The empirical risk, based on a training sample $\{(x_i, y_i)\}_{i=1}^{n}$, is given by:

$$R_{\text{emp}}(h) = \frac{1}{n} \sum_{i=1}^{n} L(h(x_i), y_i)$$

The challenge in statistical learning is controlling the complexity of $\mathcal{H}$ to ensure that the empirical risk is a good approximation of the expected risk, usually requiring regularization techniques. Under the Probably Approximately Correct (PAC) framework, one seeks to derive bounds on the generalization error that hold with high probability, typically expressed via the VC dimension or Rademacher complexity.

Functional Analysis in Neural Networks

Functional analysis plays a crucial role in understanding the properties of neural networks, particularly through operators and functional spaces. Consider a neural network as an operator $\mathcal{N} \colon \mathcal{V} \to \mathcal{W}$ mapping elements from space $\mathcal{V}$, such as the space of input signals, to a space $\mathcal{W}$, the space of outputs. Understanding continuity and boundedness is essential since:

$$\|\mathcal{N}(v)\|_{\mathcal{W}} \leq C\|v\|_{\mathcal{V}}$$

for all $v \in \mathcal{V}$ with a constant C. The parameters of the network often lie in a high-dimensional space that necessitates the study of convergence properties and stability of functional sequences, calling forth the Sobolev spaces as useful tools.

A neural network's ability to approximate functions within these spaces can be examined through the lens of universal approximation theorems, with networks being dense in specific functional spaces. The function spaces such as L^p and C^k spaces play instrumental roles in analyzing the approximation capacity and the characteristics of the functions represented by neural networks.

Information Theory in Neural Networks

Information theory provides insights into the efficiency of neural networks in encoding and transmitting information. Central to this is the concept of mutual information $I(X;Y)$ between an input variable X and output variable Y:

$$I(X;Y) = H(Y) - H(Y|X)$$

where $H(Y)$ is the entropy of Y and $H(Y|X)$ is the conditional entropy. Maximizing mutual information can be associated with the objective of achieving a compact and informative representation of data. Neural networks often exploit this through layers acting as information bottlenecks, attempting to balance compression and preservation of relevant information for predictions.

The information bottleneck method aims to find a representation T that maximizes information about the target Y while being minimally informative about the input X. This is typically formalized by:

$$\min I(X;T) - \beta I(T;Y)$$

where β is a Lagrange multiplier balancing the trade-off between compression and prediction.

1 Information Flow in Deep Networks

Deep neural networks are often viewed through the lens of information processing systems. Each layer can be thought of as a transformation of information, refining the representation towards achieving more separable and meaningful features at higher layers. Theoretical results often utilize the concept of Shannon's channel capacity to understand the limits of what can be achieved by a given network architecture in terms of information flow and error-free representation.

Python Code Snippet

Below is a Python code snippet that encompasses the core computational elements based on the theoretical frameworks discussed in this chapter, including implementations for statistical learning theory, functional analysis, and information theory concepts applied to neural networks.

```python
import numpy as np
from scipy.integrate import quad
from scipy.stats import entropy

# Statistical Learning Theory: Empirical and Expected Risk
def empirical_risk(h, X, Y, loss_func):
    '''
    Calculate empirical risk based on a hypothesis and a dataset.
    :param h: Hypothesis function.
    :param X: Feature set.
    :param Y: Target values.
    :param loss_func: Loss function.
    :return: Empirical risk.
    '''
    return np.mean([loss_func(h(x), y) for x, y in zip(X, Y)])
```

11

```python
def expected_risk(h, X_domain, Y_domain, loss_func, prob_dist):
    '''
    Calculate expected risk based on a hypothesis and probability
    ↪ distribution.
    :param h: Hypothesis function.
    :param X_domain: X domain for integration.
    :param Y_domain: Y domain for integration.
    :param loss_func: Loss function.
    :param prob_dist: Joint probability distribution function.
    :return: Expected risk.
    '''
    integrand = lambda x, y: loss_func(h(x), y) * prob_dist(x, y)
    return quad(lambda x: quad(lambda y: integrand(x, y),
    ↪ *Y_domain)[0], *X_domain)[0]

# Functional Analysis: Neural Network as Operator
class NeuralNetworkOperator:
    def __init__(self, weights, biases):
        self.weights = weights
        self.biases = biases

    def apply(self, v):
        '''
        Apply neural network as an operator.
        :param v: Input vector from space V.
        :return: Output vector in space W.
        '''
        return np.dot(self.weights, v) + self.biases

    def is_bounded(self):
        '''
        Check for boundedness of the operator.
        :return: Boolean indicating boundedness.
        '''
        # Example condition for boundedness
        return np.linalg.norm(self.weights) < np.inf

# Information Theory: Mutual Information
def mutual_information(X, Y):
    '''
    Calculate mutual information I(X; Y) between input X and output
    ↪ Y.
    :param X: Input data distribution.
    :param Y: Output data distribution.
    :return: Mutual information.
    '''
    H_Y = entropy(Y)
    H_Y_given_X = np.mean([entropy(y | x) for x, y in zip(X, Y)])
    return H_Y - H_Y_given_X

def information_bottleneck(X, T, Y, beta):
    '''
    Perform information bottleneck method.
```

```
    :param X: Input data.
    :param T: Representation.
    :param Y: Target data.
    :param beta: Trade-off parameter.
    :return: Information bottleneck value.
    '''
    I_X_T = mutual_information(X, T)
    I_T_Y = mutual_information(T, Y)
    return I_X_T - beta * I_T_Y

# Example Usage
def loss_function(y_pred, y_true):
    return (y_pred - y_true) ** 2

# Dummy probability distribution function
probability_distribution = lambda x, y: 1 / (1 + np.exp(-x * y))

# Define hypothesis as neural network operator
nn_operator = NeuralNetworkOperator(weights=np.array([0.5, 0.5]),
↪   biases=np.array([0.1]))

# Dummy datasets
X_sample = [0.5, 0.2, 0.9]
Y_sample = [0.4, 0.1, 0.8]

# Calculate risks
emp_risk = empirical_risk(nn_operator.apply, X_sample, Y_sample,
↪   loss_function)
exp_risk = expected_risk(nn_operator.apply, (0, 1), (0, 1),
↪   loss_function, probability_distribution)

# Calculate mutual information and information bottleneck
mutual_info = mutual_information(X_sample, Y_sample)
info_bottleneck_value = information_bottleneck(X_sample, Y_sample,
↪   Y_sample, beta=1.0)

print("Empirical Risk:", emp_risk)
print("Expected Risk:", exp_risk)
print("Mutual Information:", mutual_info)
print("Information Bottleneck Value:", info_bottleneck_value)
```

This code defines several key functions and classes that help capture essential theoretical concepts discussed in this chapter:

- `empirical_risk` and `expected_risk` functions compute empirical and expected risk, respectively, for given hypotheses.

- `NeuralNetworkOperator` class encapsulates neural networks as mathematical operators, examining properties like boundedness.

- `mutual_information` calculates the mutual information between input and output distributions.

- `information_bottleneck` evaluates the information bottleneck value to optimize the trade-off between data compression and relevancy.

These implementations provide a practical connection between theory and code, enabling precise control and evaluation of neural network performance through these advanced methodologies.

Chapter 2

Universal Approximation Theorems

Universal Approximation Properties

The fundamental principle of universal approximation posits that neural networks with sufficient capacity can approximate any function to arbitrary precision, given suitable conditions. A paramount result in this field is the Universal Approximation Theorem (UAP) which establishes the efficacy of feedforward neural networks with a single hidden layer in representing continuous functions defined on compact subsets of $\mathbb{R}^n$.

$$f\colon \mathbb{R}^n \to \mathbb{R} \quad \text{can be approximated by} \quad \hat{f}(x) = \sum_{i=1}^{m} \alpha_i \sigma(w_i^T x + b_i)$$

$$(2.1)$$

where σ is a non-linear activation function, typically chosen to be sigmoidal, and m is the number of neurons in the hidden layer. The theorem does not impose restrictions on the structure of σ beyond being non-constant, bounded, and continuous.

Role of Activation Functions

The choice of activation functions σ critically affects the universality of the network. Critical studies have shown that activation functions such as the logistic sigmoid and hyperbolic tangent satisfy the conditions for universality. The ReLU (Rectified Linear Unit), defined as:

$$\sigma(x) = \max(0, x) \tag{2.2}$$

also demonstrates powerful approximation capabilities, particularly in deep architectures despite lacking boundedness, leveraging its piecewise linear nature.

1 Conditions for Approximation

For a neural network to achieve universal approximation, sufficient conditions include:
1. The representation of the function σ in terms of simple elementary functions. 2. Existence of parameters α_i, w_i, b_i such that the approximation error is minimized according to some norm, typically the L^1 or L^2 norm.

The error of approximation can be expressed as:

$$\|f - \hat{f}\| < \epsilon \tag{2.3}$$

for any small $\epsilon > 0$.

Convergence and Capacity Analysis

The capacity of a neural network, which determines its power to approximate functions, is linked to its VC (Vapnik–Chervonenkis) dimension. It quantifies the model complexity based on the maximum number of samples that can be shattered. Formally, the VC dimension d_{VC} links to the number of parameters:

$$d_{VC} = O(W \log W) \tag{2.4}$$

where W is the number of weights in the network. A higher VC dimension generally implies a richer hypothesis space, enhancing approximating abilities but introducing the risk of overfitting.

1   Degree of Approximation

The degree to which a function can be approximated by a neural network relates to the width and depth of the network. The interplay of these architectural choices affects the speed of convergence to the target function. Increasing the depth can exponentially improve representation power, pivotal in the context of deep learning paradigms.

The approximation rate can be linked to the smoothness of the function being approximated:

$$\text{Approximation Rate} \sim O(n^{-\frac{s}{d}}) \qquad (2.5)$$

where s denotes the smoothness degree and d represents the dimension of input space.

Implications and Theoretical Insights

While the UAP establishes the potential of neural networks in function approximation, it does not provide guidance on the network parameter selection for practical applications. Limitations like nondeterministic nature of training dynamics in neural network parameter spaces and the presence of local optima highlight challenges in exploiting these capabilities fully. Practical implementations heavily rely on empirical heuristics augmenting theoretical assurances.

The study of universal approximation theorems forms a theoretical backbone urging further exploration into more refined models and architectures enhancing practical implementations of neural networks in diverse application domains.

Python Code Snippet

Below is a Python code snippet that encompasses the core computational elements related to universal approximation theorems in neural networks. It includes implementations for function approximation, activation function application, and certain analytics related to network capacity and convergence.

```python
import numpy as np
from scipy.special import expit  # Sigmoid function
```

```python
def neural_network_approximation(x, weights, biases,
↪   activation_func):
    '''
    Approximates a function using a simple feedforward neural
    ↪   network.
    :param x: Input vector.
    :param weights: Weights matrix for the hidden layer.
    :param biases: Bias vector for the hidden layer.
    :param activation_func: Activation function to apply.
    :return: Approximated function value.
    '''
    z = np.dot(weights, x) + biases
    return np.sum(activation_func(z))

def sigmoid_activation(x):
    '''
    Sigmoid activation function.
    :param x: Input value(s).
    :return: Output after applying sigmoid function.
    '''
    return expit(x)

def relu_activation(x):
    '''
    ReLU activation function.
    :param x: Input value(s).
    :return: Output after applying ReLU function.
    '''
    return np.maximum(0, x)

def approximation_error(target_function, approximation_function,
↪   inputs, weights, biases, activation_func):
    '''
    Calculate the error of approximation between the target and
    ↪   approximated function.
    :param target_function: The actual function to approximate.
    :param approximation_function: The neural approximation
    ↪   function.
    :param inputs: A set of input vectors.
    :param weights: Weights matrix for the network.
    :param biases: Bias vector for the network.
    :param activation_func: Activation function used in
    ↪   approximation.
    :return: Sum of approximation errors.
    '''
    errors = []
    for x in inputs:
        target_value = target_function(x)
        approx_value = approximation_function(x, weights, biases,
        ↪   activation_func)
        errors.append(np.abs(target_value - approx_value))
    return np.sum(errors)
```

```python
def calculate_vc_dimension(weights):
    '''
    Calculate an approximation of the VC dimension for the neural
    ↪  network.
    :param weights: Total number of weights in the network.
    :return: Approximated VC dimension.
    '''
    return weights * np.log2(weights)

# Example usage

# Define a target function: f(x) = 2x + 3
target_func = lambda x: 2 * x + 3

# Simple input setup
X = np.array([1, 2, 3, 4, 5])

# Network parameters
weights_example = np.array([[0.5, -0.5, 0.3]])  # Example weights
biases_example = np.array([0.1])  # Example biases

# Calculate approximation errors using sigmoid activation
error_sigmoid = approximation_error(target_func,
↪  neural_network_approximation, X, weights_example,
↪  biases_example, sigmoid_activation)

# Calculate approximation errors using ReLU activation
error_relu = approximation_error(target_func,
↪  neural_network_approximation, X, weights_example,
↪  biases_example, relu_activation)

# Display results
print("Approximation Error with Sigmoid:", error_sigmoid)
print("Approximation Error with ReLU:", error_relu)

# Calculate VC dimension
vc_dim = calculate_vc_dimension(len(weights_example.flatten()))
print("VC Dimension Approximation:", vc_dim)
```

This code defines several key functions necessary for understanding the approximation capabilities of neural networks, as discussed in the universal approximation theorem:

- **neural_network_approximation** simulates a neural network function approximation with configurable parameters.

- **sigmoid_activation** and **relu_activation** provide two common activation functions suitable for evaluating universality.

- **approximation_error** calculates the approximation error for a given target function, which is vital for understanding the performance.

- `calculate_vc_dimension` estimates the VC dimension, linking the theoretical considerations about capacity to network design.

The script demonstrates using two activations and provides an illustrative calculation of the VC dimension, reflecting the principles of network capacity and analysis.

Chapter 3

Depth vs. Width Trade-offs

Expressive Power of Neural Networks

The expressive power of a neural network refers to its ability to represent various functions. Two principal architectural features—depth (number of layers) and width (number of neurons per layer)—play a critical role in dictating this power. The increased depth allows networks to compose simple functions into more complex representations through hierarchical feature extraction.

The formal expression of a feedforward neural network with n layers can be written as a function composition:

$$f(x) = f^{(n)}(f^{(n-1)}(\cdots f^{(1)}(x) \cdots))$$

where $f^{(l)}$ represents the transformation at the l-th layer, typically modeled as:

$$f^{(l)}(x) = \sigma(W^{(l)}x + b^{(l)})$$

with $W^{(l)}$ denoting the weight matrix and $b^{(l)}$ the bias vector for the l-th layer, and σ being a non-linear activation function.

Trade-offs in Network Depth

1 Benefits of Depth

The primary advantage of depth is captured in the concept of network hierarchy, enhancing both representational efficiency and function complexity:

1. **Hierarchical Feature Learning**: Deeper networks can learn abstract representations by gradually extracting hierarchically structured features. 2. **Expressive Richness**: Given an exponentially growing expressive capacity, deep networks often approximate complex functions with fewer parameters than their shallow counterparts. 3. **Universal Approximation and Depth**: For a given function class, depth can often reduce the requirement of network width, drawing from the universality results:

$$\texttt{Depth can reduce parameter requirement} \implies \prod_{l=1}^{n} \texttt{Width of layer } l$$

This links the function composition based on the hierarchy to attain such expressiveness exponentially.

2 Challenges of Deep Architectures

However, depth introduces significant training challenges:

1. **Vanishing/Exploding Gradients**: As networks deepen, gradients either diminish or grow exponentially, leading to convergence issues during training where activations and gradients are expressed as:

$$\frac{\partial L}{\partial W^{(l)}} = \delta^{(l)} x^{(l-1)T}$$

The derivative $\delta^{(l)}$ tends to vanish or explode if not controlled by techniques such as batch normalization.

2. **Optimization Complexity**: Increased parameter space and intricate loss landscapes pose difficulties for optimization algorithms, often resulting in getting trapped in local minima or saddle points.

Influence of Network Width

1 Advantages of Increased Width

Width, in contrast, provides alternative benefits, especially in architectures where deeper hierarchies are not essential:

1. **Linear Region Approximation**: Wider networks significantly enhance the linear region coverage, a critical aspect when dealing with non-linear activation functions like ReLU.

2. **Neural Tangent Kernel (NTK) Behavior**: Infinite width bridges deep learning with kernel methods, expressed as the NTK regime where:

$$\lim_{m \to \infty} f(x) = \sum_{i=1}^{m} \alpha_i \texttt{ReLU}(w_i^T x)$$

depicts this approximation paradigm, where layer width $m \to \infty$ equates network behavior to a stationary kernel function.

2 Constraints and Limits of Width

Despite its benefits, increasing width presents challenges:

1. **Practical Scalability**: Hardware limitations can restrict feasible width, alongside increased computational overhead encompassing:

$$O(n \cdot \texttt{Width}^2)$$

due to matrix multiplications growing quadratically with layer size.

2. **Diminishing Returns**: Beyond a threshold, additional neurons offer marginal gains in function approximation, aligning with the curse of dimensionality that reflects in increased training samples needed beyond lower bounds.

Balancing Depth and Width

The optimal design of a neural architecture often involves balancing depth versus width to maximize generalization while minimizing complexity and computational constraints.

1. **Hybrid Architectures**: Architectures such as ResNets and DenseNets effectively leverage both increased depth and strategic width to improve learning dynamics and stability.

2. **Empirical Determination**: Experimentation often dictates the optimal structure governed by application-specific heuristics, empirical testing, and performance benchmarking across varying tasks and datasets.

The correct calibration aligns with both empirical observations and theoretically guided insights to design networks adapting to domain-specific demands in terms of interpretability, scalability, and computational efficiency, ultimately governed by learning dynamics encoded within the function:

$$\min_\theta L(f(x; \theta), y)$$

where θ encapsulates all tunable parameters, integrating both depth and width considerations across neural network scaffolding.

Python Code Snippet

Below is a Python code snippet that encapsulates the core computational elements relevant to the expressed theoretical concepts of depth vs. width trade-offs in neural networks. It includes implementations for functions, evaluations of network properties, and optimizations discussed in the chapter.

```python
import numpy as np

# Function for the neural network layer transformation
def layer_transformation(x, W, b, activation_func):
    '''
    Calculate layer transformation with weights, biases, and
    ↪ activation.
    :param x: Input to the layer.
    :param W: Weight matrix.
    :param b: Bias vector.
    :param activation_func: Non-linear activation function.
    :return: Transformed output after applying activation.
    '''
    return activation_func(np.dot(W, x) + b)

# Example of ReLU activation function
def relu(x):
    return np.maximum(0, x)

# Depth vs. Width Trade-offs Representation
def neural_network_forward_pass(layers_config, x):
    '''
    Perform a forward pass through a neural network.
```

```python
    :param layers_config: Configuration of layers with weights and
    ↪    biases.
    :param x: Input vector.
    :return: Final output after forward propagation.
    '''
    for W, b, activation in layers_config:
        x = layer_transformation(x, W, b, activation)
    return x

# Example layer configurations with random weights and biases
layers_config = [
    (np.random.rand(16, 8), np.random.rand(16), relu),   # Layer 1
    (np.random.rand(8, 16), np.random.rand(8), relu),    # Layer 2
    (np.random.rand(4, 8), np.random.rand(4), relu)      # Layer 3
]

# Initial input
x = np.random.rand(8)

# Running forward pass
output = neural_network_forward_pass(layers_config, x)
print("Output of the network:", output)

# Function to calculate width-based properties
def neural_tangent_kernel_approximation(W, x):
    '''
    Illustrates Neural Tangent Kernel (NTK) behavior approximation.
    :param W: Weight matrix with large width.
    :param x: Input vector.
    :return: NTK approximation result.
    '''
    return np.sum(np.maximum(0, np.dot(W, x)))

# Infinite width approximation using NTK
def infinite_width_approximation(x, num_neurons=10000):
    '''
    Approximate behavior of network at infinite width using NTK.
    :param x: Input vector.
    :param num_neurons: Number of neurons to approximate infinite
    ↪    width.
    :return: Resulting approximation.
    '''
    W_inf = np.random.randn(num_neurons, x.shape[0])
    return neural_tangent_kernel_approximation(W_inf, x)

# Example usage
ntk_result = infinite_width_approximation(x)
print("NTK Approximation at large width:", ntk_result)

# Balancing depth and width
def optimize_architecture(layers_config, maximize_depth=True):
    '''
    Optimize neural network architecture parameters.
```

```
:param layers_config: Configuration of layers.
:param maximize_depth: Boolean indicating depth vs width focus.
:return: Optimized architecture configuration.
'''
# Placeholder adaptation strategy
if maximize_depth:
    # Example: Add more layers or increase layer depth
    layers_config.append((np.random.rand(2, 4),
    ↪  np.random.rand(2), relu))
return layers_config

# Adjusting architecture
optimized_layers = optimize_architecture(layers_config,
↪  maximize_depth=True)
print("Optimized architecture with additional depth:",
↪  optimized_layers)
```

This code comprises essential components to simulate neural network behaviors that align with the theoretical discussions of depth versus width trade-offs:

- `layer_transformation` transforms inputs through the application of weights, biases, and activation functions.

- `neural_network_forward_pass` executes forward propagation through a configured network, demonstrating the composition of functions across layers.

- `neural_tangent_kernel_approximation` approximates the NTK behavior, highlighting the relationship between infinite width networks and kernel methods.

- `infinite_width_approximation` simulates the approximation effect of networks with increasingly large widths.

- `optimize_architecture` illustrates a hypothetical approach to adjusting architecture balancing between depth and width for optimized network performance.

These elements provide a basis for experimentation and deeper understanding of the architectural implications captured within neural network designs.

Chapter 4

Optimization Landscapes and Geometry

Optimization Landscapes in Neural Networks

The optimization landscape of neural networks is characterized by the high-dimensional non-convex function represented by the loss function. This function, $L(\theta)$, is parameterized by θ, which spans the weights and biases of the network. The topology of these landscapes influences the success of training algorithms and their convergence properties.

The loss function can be expressed as:

$$L(\theta) = \frac{1}{N} \sum_{i=1}^{N} \ell(f(x_i; \theta), y_i)$$

where N is the number of training samples, $f(x_i; \theta)$ is the prediction of the network for input x_i, and ℓ is the chosen loss measure, such as cross-entropy or mean squared error.

Critical Points in Neural Networks

Critical points in the loss landscape, including minima, maxima, and saddle points, play a pivotal role in gradient-based optimization. A critical point θ^* satisfies:

$$\nabla L(\theta^*) = 0$$

where ∇L denotes the gradient vector of the loss function with respect to the parameters θ.

1 Minima

Local minima θ^* are characterized by $\nabla^2 L(\theta^*)$, the Hessian matrix, being positive semi-definite, i.e., all eigenvalues $\lambda_i \geq 0$. The presence of multiple local minima is attributed to the complex hierarchical nature of neural network functions:

$$\theta^* \text{ is a local minimum if } \nabla^2 L(\theta^*) \succeq 0$$

2 Saddle Points

Saddle points arise frequently in high-dimensional parameter spaces of neural networks. They are characterized by a Hessian matrix with both positive and negative eigenvalues, indicating directions of concave and convex behavior:

$$\exists \lambda_i : \lambda_i < 0 \rightarrow \theta^* \text{ is a saddle point}$$

Given the prevalence of saddle points more than local minima in high dimensions, understanding their properties assists in optimization algorithm design.

Saddle Points and The Impact on Training Dynamics

Training dynamics of neural networks, particularly with gradient descent-based methods, are significantly affected by saddle points. These points slow convergence since gradients in directions of negative curvature are typically non-zero, complicating the escape during optimization.

The dynamics near a saddle point can be modeled using a second-order Taylor expansion:

$$L(\theta^* + \Delta\theta) \approx L(\theta^*) + \Delta\theta^T \nabla L(\theta^*) + \frac{1}{2}\Delta\theta^T \nabla^2 L(\theta^*)\Delta\theta$$

with alterations in $\Delta\theta$ governed largely by second-order terms in the vicinity of a saddle.

Geometric Structure of Loss Landscapes

Understanding the geometry of the loss functions enhances intuitions for algorithmic developments. The curvature and shape defined by the Hessian enable techniques like second-order optimization to potentially mitigate saddle point problems.

1 Role of Curvature

The curvature at a point is described by the eigenvalues of the Hessian matrix:
- Positive curvature, $\lambda_i > 0$, indicates a local convex region. - Negative curvature, $\lambda_i < 0$, implies concavity.

This curvature information is exploited in algorithms such as Newton's method, where an update is given by:

$$\theta \leftarrow \theta - \alpha(\nabla^2 L(\theta))^{-1}\nabla L(\theta)$$

2 Landscapes in Different Neural Architectures

Different architectures, including convolutional and recurrent networks, generate uniquely structured optimization landscapes, contingent on weight-sharing and sequential modeling constraints, respectively.

For instance, in convolutional networks, weight-sharing introduces a structure that considerably reduces the effective parameter space, impacting the curvature and symmetry properties:

$$\theta_{\text{conv}} \ll \theta_{\text{ff}}$$

where θ_{conv} and θ_{ff} correspond to parameter spaces of convolutional and fully connected networks.

These landscape characteristics motivate the development of specialized optimization strategies tailored to harness these architectural dimensions, facilitating more effective and efficient neural network training outcomes.

Python Code Snippet

Below is a Python code snippet that encompasses the core computational elements of neural network optimization landscape analysis including the calculation of critical points, Hessians, and optimization techniques using second-order methods.

```python
import numpy as np
from scipy.optimize import minimize

def loss_function(parameters, data, labels):
    '''
    Calculate loss for given parameters.
    :param parameters: Neural network weights and biases vector.
    :param data: Input data samples.
    :param labels: True labels for data.
    :return: Computed loss.
    '''
    predictions = predict(data, parameters)
    return np.mean(np.square(predictions - labels))  # Mean squared
    ↪  error

def predict(data, parameters):
    '''
    Placeholder function for predicted outputs.
    :param data: Input data samples.
    :param parameters: Model parameters.
    :return: Predicted data.
    '''
    # Mock prediction function
    return data @ parameters  # Assuming linear model for
    ↪  demonstration

def compute_gradient(loss_fn, parameters, data, labels):
    '''
    Compute gradient of the loss function with respect to
    ↪  parameters.
    :param loss_fn: Loss function.
    :param parameters: Parameters for which gradient is calculated.
    :param data: Input data samples.
    :param labels: True labels for data.
    :return: Gradient vector.
    '''
    epsilon = 1e-5
```

```python
        grad = np.zeros_like(parameters)
        for i in range(len(parameters)):
            params_plus = np.copy(parameters)
            params_minus = np.copy(parameters)
            params_plus[i] += epsilon
            params_minus[i] -= epsilon
            grad[i] = (loss_fn(params_plus, data, labels) -
             ↪  loss_fn(params_minus, data, labels)) / (2 * epsilon)
        return grad

def compute_hessian(loss_fn, parameters, data, labels):
    '''
    Compute Hessian matrix of the loss function.
    :param loss_fn: Loss function.
    :param parameters: Parameters for which Hessian is calculated.
    :param data: Input data samples.
    :param labels: True labels for data.
    :return: Hessian matrix.
    '''

    epsilon = 1e-5
    num_params = len(parameters)
    hessian = np.zeros((num_params, num_params))
    for i in range(num_params):
        for j in range(num_params):
            params_ij = np.copy(parameters)
            params_ij[[i, j]] += epsilon
            hessian[i, j] = (loss_fn(params_ij, data, labels)
                            - loss_fn(np.copy(parameters), data,
                             ↪  labels)) / (epsilon ** 2)
    return hessian

def train_model(data, labels, initial_parameters):
    '''
    Train the neural network model using second-order optimization.
    :param data: Input data samples.
    :param labels: True labels for data.
    :param initial_parameters: Initial model parameters.
    :return: Optimized parameters.
    '''

    def objective_fn(params):
        return loss_function(params, data, labels)

    result = minimize(objective_fn, initial_parameters,
     ↪  method='Newton-CG',
                        jac=lambda p: compute_gradient(objective_fn,
                         ↪  p, data, labels),
                        hess=lambda p: compute_hessian(objective_fn,
                         ↪  p, data, labels))
    return result.x

# Example of usage
data_samples = np.random.rand(100, 5)  # 100 samples, 5 features
 ↪  each
```

```
true_labels = np.random.rand(100)
initial_params = np.random.rand(5)

optimized_params = train_model(data_samples, true_labels,
↪    initial_params)

print("Optimized Parameters:", optimized_params)
```

This code defines several key functions necessary for the investigation and analysis of optimization landscapes in neural networks:

- `loss_function` computes the loss value given the model parameters and data. It uses mean squared error as an example loss.

- `predict` acts as a placeholder for demonstrating model prediction, assuming a simple linear transformation.

- `compute_gradient` calculates the gradient of the loss with respect to model parameters using finite differences method.

- `compute_hessian` estimates the Hessian matrix of the loss function, illustrating second-order derivative calculations.

- `train_model` employs second-order optimization techniques using gradient and Hessian information for parameter tuning.

The final block of code provides examples of computing these elements using dummy data and showcases parameter optimization using the Newton-CG method.

Chapter 5

Advanced Gradient-Based Optimization Methods

Second-Order Optimization Methods

Second-order optimization methods leverage the curvature information of the loss surface to guide the search for optimal parameters more efficiently. These methods utilize the Hessian matrix, $\nabla^2 L(\theta)$, to provide a quadratic approximation of the loss function. The Newton-Raphson update is given by:

$$\theta_{k+1} = \theta_k - (\nabla^2 L(\theta_k))^{-1} \nabla L(\theta_k)$$

where θ_k represents the current parameter estimate, $\nabla L(\theta_k)$ is the gradient, and $\nabla^2 L(\theta_k)$ is the Hessian matrix evaluated at θ_k.

1   Challenges with Second-Order Methods

The computational expense of calculating and storing the Hessian, as well as inverting it, constrains the direct applicability of second-order methods in large-scale neural networks. Approximations like limited-memory Broyden–Fletcher–Goldfarb–Shanno (L-BFGS) seek to reduce these costs by estimating curvature information without constructing the full Hessian.

Adaptive Learning Rate Strategies

Adaptive learning rate methods adjust the step size dynamically based on the observed gradients during training. These strategies aim to converge efficiently by tuning learning rates with respect to the scale and variability of the parameters.

1 Adagrad, RMSProp, and Adam

Adagrad adapts the learning rate by scaling it inversely with the cumulative sum of squared gradients:

$$\theta_{t+1} = \theta_t - \frac{\eta}{\sqrt{\sum_{i=1}^{t} g_i^2 + \epsilon}} \cdot g_t$$

where $g_t = \nabla L(\theta_t)$, η is the initial learning rate, and ϵ is a small constant to prevent division by zero.

RMSProp modifies Adagrad by utilizing an exponentially decaying average of past squared gradients:

$$E[g^2]_t = \gamma E[g^2]_{t-1} + (1 - \gamma)g_t^2$$

$$\theta_{t+1} = \theta_t - \frac{\eta}{\sqrt{E[g^2]_t + \epsilon}} \cdot g_t$$

where γ is the decay rate.

Adam combines the benefits of RMSProp and momentum methods, integrating first and second moment estimates:

$$m_t = \beta_1 m_{t-1} + (1 - \beta_1)g_t$$

$$v_t = \beta_2 v_{t-1} + (1 - \beta_2)g_t^2$$

Bias-corrected estimates are then used to update the parameters:

$$\hat{m}_t = \frac{m_t}{1 - \beta_1^t}, \quad \hat{v}_t = \frac{v_t}{1 - \beta_2^t}$$

$$\theta_{t+1} = \theta_t - \frac{\eta}{\sqrt{\hat{v}_t} + \epsilon} \cdot \hat{m}_t$$

Theoretical Convergence Properties

Analysis of convergence rates provides insight into the effectiveness and robustness of optimization algorithms. For strongly convex functions, second-order methods can achieve superlinear convergence. Adaptive methods guarantee convergence with sublinear rates under convexity assumptions.

1 Strongly Convex Functions

If the loss function is strongly convex with parameter $\mu > 0$, and Lipschitz continuous with constant L, gradient descent's convergence rate is defined by:

$$\|\theta_k - \theta^*\| \leq \left(1 - \frac{2\mu L}{\mu + L}\right)^k \|\theta_0 - \theta^*\|$$

Strong convexity ensures a unique global minimum, guiding optimizations efficiently towards θ^*.

2 Adaptive Method Guarantees

Adaptive optimization provides theoretical guarantees under convexity with conditions such as diminishing learning rates or accumulating squared gradient history. Adam, for instance, ensures practical convergence by adaptively updating parameter-specific learning rates, facilitating faster convergence on large, sparse datasets.

Adaptive techniques offer particular robustness to hyperparameter selection, advantageous in environments where expert tuning is infeasible.

Python Code Snippet

Below is a Python code snippet that encompasses the core computational elements of second-order optimization methods, adaptive learning rate strategies, and theoretical convergence properties as discussed in this chapter.

```python
import numpy as np

def newton_raphson_update(theta_k, grad, hessian_inv):
    '''
    Perform a Newton-Raphson update step.
```

```
    :param theta_k: Current parameter estimate.
    :param grad: Gradient evaluated at current parameters.
    :param hessian_inv: Inverse of Hessian at current parameters.
    :return: Updated parameter.
    '''
    return theta_k - np.dot(hessian_inv, grad)

def lbfgs_update(theta_k, grad_func, m=10):
    '''
    Approximates Hessian using limited-memory BFGS update.
    :param theta_k: Current parameter estimate.
    :param grad_func: Gradient function.
    :param m: Memory parameter (number of corrections to store).
    :return: Updated parameters.
    '''
    q = grad_func(theta_k)
    alpha = []
    rho = []
    s = []
    y = []

    for i in range(m):
        s_i = np.random.randn(*theta_k.shape)  # Random
          ↪ approximation of s
        y_i = grad_func(theta_k + s_i) - q
        rho_i = 1.0 / (np.dot(y_i, s_i))
        rho.append(rho_i)
        alpha_i = rho_i * np.dot(s_i, q)
        alpha.append(alpha_i)
        q = q - alpha_i * y_i
        s.append(s_i)
        y.append(y_i)

    r = np.random.randn(*q.shape)  # Random initialization for r
    for i in reversed(range(m)):
        beta = rho[i] * np.dot(y[i], r)
        r = r + s[i] * (alpha[i] - beta)

    return theta_k - r

def adagrad(theta_t, grad_t, eta=0.01, epsilon=1e-8):
    '''
    Adagrad optimization step.
    :param theta_t: Current parameter estimate.
    :param grad_t: Gradient at current parameters.
    :param eta: Learning rate.
    :param epsilon: Smoothing term.
    :return: Updated parameters.
    '''
    grad_squared = grad_t ** 2
    sum_grad_squared = np.sum(grad_squared)
    return theta_t - (eta / (np.sqrt(sum_grad_squared) + epsilon)) *
      ↪ grad_t
```

```python
def rmsprop(theta_t, grad_t, cache, eta=0.001, decay_rate=0.9,
↪    epsilon=1e-8):
    '''
    RMSProp optimization step.
    :param theta_t: Current parameter estimate.
    :param grad_t: Gradient at current parameters.
    :param cache: Cache storing squared gradients.
    :return: Updated parameters.
    '''
    cache = decay_rate * cache + (1 - decay_rate) * grad_t ** 2
    return theta_t - (eta / (np.sqrt(cache) + epsilon)) * grad_t,
↪    cache

def adam(theta_t, grad_t, m_t, v_t, t, eta=0.001, beta1=0.9,
↪    beta2=0.999, epsilon=1e-8):
    '''
    Adam optimization step.
    :param theta_t: Current parameter estimates.
    :param grad_t: Gradient at current parameters.
    :param m_t: First moment vector.
    :param v_t: Second moment vector.
    :param t: Time step.
    :return: Updated parameters and moments.
    '''
    m_t = beta1 * m_t + (1 - beta1) * grad_t
    v_t = beta2 * v_t + (1 - beta2) * (grad_t ** 2)

    m_t_hat = m_t / (1 - beta1 ** t)
    v_t_hat = v_t / (1 - beta2 ** t)

    theta_t = theta_t - (eta / (np.sqrt(v_t_hat) + epsilon)) *
↪    m_t_hat
    return theta_t, m_t, v_t

# Example of a strongly convex function
def strongly_convex_function(theta, mu=0.1, L=1.0):
    '''
    Computes descent step for a strongly convex function.
    :param theta: Parameter estimate.
    :param mu: Strong convexity constant.
    :param L: Lipschitz constant.
    :return: Descent step size.
    '''
    return (1 - 2*mu*L/(mu+L)) * np.linalg.norm(theta)

# Example of using the Adam optimizer
theta = np.random.randn(10)
grad = np.random.randn(10)
m = np.zeros_like(theta)
v = np.zeros_like(theta)
cache = np.zeros_like(theta)
t = 1
```

```
# Performing a parameter update using Newton-Raphson, Adagrad,
↪   RMSProp and Adam
hessian_inv = np.linalg.inv(np.random.rand(10, 10))   # Dummy inverse
↪   Hessian for demonstration

theta_newton = newton_raphson_update(theta, grad, hessian_inv)
theta_lbfgs = lbfgs_update(theta, lambda x: np.random.randn(10))
theta_adagrad = adagrad(theta, grad)
theta_rmsprop, cache = rmsprop(theta, grad, cache)
theta_adam, m, v = adam(theta, grad, m, v, t)

# Print updated parameter estimates
print("Updated Parameters (Newton-Raphson):", theta_newton)
print("Updated Parameters (L-BFGS):", theta_lbfgs)
print("Updated Parameters (Adagrad):", theta_adagrad)
print("Updated Parameters (RMSProp):", theta_rmsprop)
print("Updated Parameters (Adam):", theta_adam)
```

This code defines key functions for optimization in neural networks:

- **newton_raphson_update**: Implements the Newton-Raphson update using the inverse Hessian.

- **lbfgs_update**: Illustrates an L-BFGS approximation for updating parameters without explicitly calculating the Hessian.

- **adagrad**: Updates parameters according to the **Adagrad** optimization strategy, adapting learning rates based on gradient history.

- **rmsprop**: Extends **Adagrad** by incorporating an exponentially decaying average of past squared gradients.

- **adam**: Combines the principles of both momentum and **RMSProp** to enable adaptive learning rates per parameter.

- **strongly_convex_function**: A helper illustrating convergence in strongly convex functions.

The provided examples demonstrate applications of each optimization method on a randomly initialized parameter vector.

Chapter 6

Generalization Theory in Deep Learning

VC Dimension and Its Relevance to Neural Networks

The Vapnik–Chervonenkis (VC) dimension is a fundamental concept in statistical learning theory, often invoked to understand the capacity of a class of functions to shatter data points. For a hypothesis class $\mathcal{H}$, the VC dimension d_{VC} is the largest number of points that can be shattered by $\mathcal{H}$. Mathematically, if there exists a set of d_{VC} data points $x_1, x_2, \ldots, x_{d_{VC}}$ such that every one of the $2^{d_{VC}}$ binary labeling of these points can be realized by some hypothesis $h \in \mathcal{H}$, then $\mathcal{H}$ is said to have VC dimension d_{VC}.

Within the context of neural networks, particularly deep networks, the VC dimension provides insight into their expressive power. For a feedforward neural network with θ parameters, with activation functions such as sigmoids, the VC dimension can scale as $\mathcal{O}(\theta \log \theta)$. This suggests that networks with a higher number of parameters possess greater capacity to fit diverse datasets. However, such large capacity can also lead to overfitting, highlighting the delicate balance between expressiveness and generalization.

Rademacher Complexity and Its Applications

Rademacher complexity offers an alternative measure of model complexity that reflects the richness of a class of functions in relation to a particular data distribution. For a sample $S = \{x_1, x_2, \ldots, x_n\}$ of size n, the empirical Rademacher complexity $\hat{\mathcal{R}}_n(\mathcal{H})$ of a hypothesis class $\mathcal{H}$ is defined as:

$$\hat{\mathcal{R}}_n(\mathcal{H}) = \mathbb{E}_\sigma \left[\sup_{h \in \mathcal{H}} \frac{1}{n} \sum_{i=1}^n \sigma_i h(x_i) \right]$$

where σ_i are i.i.d. Rademacher variables that take values $\{-1, +1\}$ with equal probability.

This metric is particularly applicable to neural networks, providing bounds on the generalization error. The empirical Rademacher complexity can be minimized during the training phase, offering an extra layer of regularization in addition to traditional methods like weight decay. For deep neural networks, the Rademacher complexity tends to increase with both the depth and width of the network, which correlates with the intuition that deeper networks can represent more complex functions.

Generalization Bounds for Deep Networks

The combination of VC dimension and Rademacher complexity provides foundational insights into the generalization potential of neural networks. A generalization error bound often incorporates both these quantities. Consider the following generalization bound for a hypothesis $h \in \mathcal{H}$:

$$\mathcal{R}(h) \leq \hat{\mathcal{R}}_S(h) + 2\hat{\mathcal{R}}_n(\mathcal{H}) + \sqrt{\frac{8\ln(2/\delta)}{n}}$$

where $\mathcal{R}(h)$ is the true risk, $\hat{\mathcal{R}}_S(h)$ is the empirical risk, and δ is a confidence parameter.

In practical scenarios for deep learning, this bound highlights the influence of empirical risk minimization, the complexity of the hypothesis class, and the size of the dataset on the overall generalization capability. For large-scale datasets common in deep learning applications, the empirical Rademacher complexity diminishes substantially, making substantial theoretical allowances for large-capacity deep neural networks.

Critiques and Limitations

Though VC dimension and Rademacher complexity are valuable tools for understanding generalization, their direct applicability to modern deep networks has limitations. The high dimensionality and non-linear nature of deep learning models challenge traditional assumptions underpinning these measures. Often, theoretical bounds provided by VC dimension are too loose to be practical, while Rademacher complexity may underestimate generalization in highly overparameterized models, such as those exceeding the number of samples.

Recent advancements suggest incorporating complexity measures that account for implicit regularization properties of optimization algorithms like stochastic gradient descent (SGD). These include stability-based bounds, which examine the sensitivity of model predictions to perturbations in training data, and PAC-Bayesian bounds, offering probabilistic guarantees. These novel approaches remain active areas of research, highlighting the need for ongoing theoretical exploration within the field of deep learning.

Python Code Snippet

Below is a Python code snippet that encompasses the core computational elements for calculating VC dimension, Rademacher complexity, and generalization bounds as well as simulating the critiques and considerations for applying these concepts to neural networks.

```python
import numpy as np

def vc_dimension(theta, scaling_factor):
    '''
    Calculate the VC dimension of a neural network.
    :param theta: Number of parameters in the network.
    :param scaling_factor: Scaling factor for the VC dimension.
    :return: VC dimension.
    '''

    return scaling_factor * theta * np.log(theta)

def empirical_rademacher_complexity(hypothesis_class, sample_size):
```

```python
    '''
    Calculate the empirical Rademacher complexity of a neural
    ↪   network.
    :param hypothesis_class: Function class representing the neural
    ↪   network.
    :param sample_size: Size of the sample.
    :return: Rademacher complexity.
    '''
    sigma = np.random.choice([-1, 1], size=sample_size)
    return np.mean([np.max([np.sum(sigma * hypothesis(x)) for
    ↪   hypothesis in hypothesis_class]) for x in
    ↪   range(sample_size)])

def generalization_error_bound(empirical_risk,
↪   rademacher_complexity, n, delta):
    '''
    Calculate the generalization error bound.
    :param empirical_risk: Empirical risk of the model.
    :param rademacher_complexity: Rademacher complexity of the
    ↪   hypothesis class.
    :param n: Size of the dataset.
    :param delta: Confidence parameter.
    :return: Generalization error bound.
    '''
    return empirical_risk + 2 * rademacher_complexity + np.sqrt((8 *
    ↪   np.log(2/delta)) / n)

def dummy_hypothesis(x):
    '''
    Dummy hypothesis function for demonstration.
    :param x: Input value.
    :return: Calculated output.
    '''
    return 0.5 * x   # Hypothetical linear relationship

# Example usage of these functions
theta = 1000
scaling_factor = 1
vc_dim = vc_dimension(theta, scaling_factor)

sample_size = 100
hypothesis_class = [dummy_hypothesis for _ in range(10)]
rademacher_complexity =
↪   empirical_rademacher_complexity(hypothesis_class, sample_size)

empirical_risk = 0.1
n = 1000
delta = 0.05
gen_error_bound = generalization_error_bound(empirical_risk,
↪   rademacher_complexity, n, delta)

print("VC Dimension:", vc_dim)
print("Rademacher Complexity:", rademacher_complexity)
```

42

```python
print("Generalization Error Bound:", gen_error_bound)

# Critiques and Limitations Handling
def stability_based_bound(data_points, sensitivity_function):
    '''
    Placeholder for stability-based bound calculation.
    :param data_points: Training data points.
    :param sensitivity_function: A function to measure sensitivity.
    :return: Stability-based bound.
    '''
    # Dummy calculation for demonstration
    return np.sum([sensitivity_function(data_point) for data_point
    ↪  in data_points]) / len(data_points)

def pac_bayesian_bound(prior, posterior, empirical_risk, data_size,
↪ complexity):
    '''
    Mock calculation of a PAC-Bayesian bound.
    :param prior: Prior distribution.
    :param posterior: Posterior distribution.
    :param empirical_risk: Observed risk.
    :param data_size: Size of the dataset.
    :param complexity: Complexity measure.
    :return: PAC-Bayesian bound.
    '''
    return empirical_risk + complexity / np.sqrt(data_size)  #
    ↪  Simplified version

# Example demonstration
data_points = np.random.rand(1000)
sensitivity_function = lambda x: x * 0.01
stability_bound = stability_based_bound(data_points,
↪  sensitivity_function)

prior = np.random.rand()
posterior = np.random.rand()
complexity = 0.1
pac_bound = pac_bayesian_bound(prior, posterior, empirical_risk,
↪  data_size=n, complexity=complexity)

print("Stability-based Bound:", stability_bound)
print("PAC-Bayesian Bound:", pac_bound)
```

This code provides a comprehensive implementation of theoretical concepts discussed in the chapter:

- `vc_dimension` function calculates the VC dimension of a neural network based on the number of parameters.

- `empirical_rademacher_complexity` computes the empirical Rademacher complexity as an indicator of function class richness.

43

- `generalization_error_bound` estimates the generalization error bound, integrating empirical risk and complexity measures.

- Considerations like `stability_based_bound` and `pac_bayesian_bound` highlight extensions and critiques of traditional methods in evaluating neural networks.

Outputs from these functions illustrate how key theoretical bounds and critiques might be evaluated practically across neural network models.

Chapter 7

Regularization Techniques and Their Theoretical Foundations

Weight Decay

Weight decay, often utilized as L_2 regularization, is a cornerstone method in mitigating overfitting in machine learning models. Formally, weight decay adds a penalty term to the loss function proportional to the square of the magnitude of the model parameters. For a given set of weights $\mathbf{w}$, the regularized loss function $\mathcal{L}_{reg}(\mathbf{w})$ is defined by

$$\mathcal{L}_{reg}(\mathbf{w}) = \mathcal{L}(\mathbf{w}) + \frac{\lambda}{2}\|\mathbf{w}\|_2^2$$

where $\mathcal{L}(\mathbf{w})$ denotes the original loss function and λ is the regularization strength. The regularization term λ modulates the trade-off between achieving a minimal empirical error and maintaining smaller weights, thereby discouraging complexity in favor of simplicity.

Deriving from the principles of regularization theory, weight decay effectively constrains the function class by limiting the norm of the weights. The constraint can be interpreted through the lens of bias-variance trade-offs, where the bias is slightly increased to achieve a more substantial reduction in variance, fostering improved generalization performance on unseen data.

Dropout Technique

Introduced as a stochastic regularization method, dropout aims to prevent co-adaptation of hidden units by randomly omitting network units during training iterations. Consider a neural network where each unit has an activation function $a_i(x)$. In dropout, each unit is retained with probability p and dropped with probability $1 - p$. The modified activations are described by

$$a_i^{drop}(x) = a_i(x) \cdot m_i$$

where m_i is a binary mask drawn from a Bernoulli distribution $\texttt{Bernoulli}(p)$. This stochasticity induces a form of model averaging by training a large ensemble composed of all possible subnetworks, each sampled by random dropout.

Theoretically, dropout can be viewed as an adaptive regularizer that implicitly applies an L_2 penalty on the weights, alongside performing implicit feature selection. The information-theoretic perspective suggests dropout enhances the network's ability to generalize by maximizing mutual information between hidden units and target outputs while minimizing irrelevant feature interference.

Data Augmentation

Data augmentation serves as a regularization technique by artificially expanding the training dataset with transformed instances. Given an original dataset $\mathcal{D} = \{(x_i, y_i)\}$, transformed samples $\mathcal{T}(x_i)$ are generated through operations such as rotations, scaling, and translations while retaining the semantic essence of the original data.

The primary equation governing data augmentation can be expressed as

$$\mathcal{L}_{aug}(\mathbf{w}) = \frac{1}{N} \sum_{i=1}^{N} \mathbb{E}_{t \sim \mathcal{T}} \left[\ell(f(t(x_i); \mathbf{w}), y_i) \right]$$

where $\ell(\cdot, \cdot)$ denotes the loss function, $f(\cdot; \mathbf{w})$ represents the model with parameters $\mathbf{w}$, and the expectation $\mathbb{E}_{t \sim \mathcal{T}}$ indicates averaging over possible transformations.

Data augmentation enhances generalization by reducing model sensitivity to input perturbations, effectively increasing the discriminatory space and the invariance of the learned representations. The augmentation strategies can be fine-tuned to enforce specific invariances desired by the application domain, such as translational or rotational invariance in image recognition tasks.

Comparison of Regularization Techniques

Regularization techniques such as weight decay, dropout, and data augmentation work synergistically to counteract overfitting by expanding the hypothesis space description, reducing network complexity, or enhancing data diversity.

While weight decay conventionally targets parameter norms, dropout offers feature-level regularization, and data augmentation addresses instance-level variability. Each method embodies unique theoretical challenges and advantages, often dictated by the model architecture and data characteristics.

Analyzing regularization from a learning theory framework highlights the balance between empirical risk and functional complexity—underscoring the necessity for diverse regularization strategies across varied learning paradigms. The intricate interplay between these techniques elucidates the resilience and adaptability of modern machine learning models in achieving robust generalization.

Python Code Snippet

Below is a Python code snippet that encompasses the core implementations of regularization techniques discussed in this chapter, including weight decay, dropout, and data augmentation.

```python
import numpy as np

def regularized_loss(original_loss, weights, lambda_):
    '''
    Compute the regularized loss with weight decay.
    :param original_loss: The loss of the model without
    ↪    regularization.
    :param weights: Model weights, typically a numpy array.
```

```python
    :param lambda_: Regularization strength.
    :return: Regularized loss value.
    '''
    l2_norm = np.sum(weights ** 2)
    return original_loss + (lambda_ / 2) * l2_norm

def apply_dropout(layer_activations, dropout_prob):
    '''
    Apply dropout to a layer during training.
    :param layer_activations: The activations of the layer (numpy
    ↪  array).
    :param dropout_prob: Probability of retaining a unit.
    :return: Modified activations after applying dropout.
    '''
    dropout_mask = np.random.binomial(1, dropout_prob,
    ↪  size=layer_activations.shape)
    return layer_activations * dropout_mask / dropout_prob

def augment_data(x, augmentation_functions):
    '''
    Apply a series of transformation functions to the data for
    ↪  augmentation.
    :param x: Original data to augment.
    :param augmentation_functions: List of functions for data
    ↪  transformations.
    :return: Augmented data.
    '''
    augmented_x = []
    for func in augmentation_functions:
        augmented_x.append(func(x))
    return np.array(augmented_x)

# Example usage
weights = np.array([1.0, -1.5, 0.5])  # Example weights of a model
original_loss = 3.0  # Example original loss
lambda_ = 0.1  # Regularization strength

# Regularized loss calculation
reg_loss = regularized_loss(original_loss, weights, lambda_)
print("Regularized Loss:", reg_loss)

# Dropout example
layer_activations = np.array([0.8, 0.5, 0.3])  # Example
↪  activations
dropout_prob = 0.5  # Probability of keeping a unit
modified_activations = apply_dropout(layer_activations,
↪  dropout_prob)
print("Activations after Dropout:", modified_activations)

# Data augmentation functions example
def rotate(x): return np.rot90(x)
def flip(x): return np.fliplr(x)
```

```
original_data = np.array([[1, 2], [3, 4]])   # Example 2D data
augmentation_funcs = [rotate, flip]

augmented_data = augment_data(original_data, augmentation_funcs)
print("Augmented Data:")
for data in augmented_data:
    print(data)
```

This code snippet encompasses the following key computational elements related to regularization techniques:

- `regularized_loss` function computes the loss incorporating weight decay L_2 regularization, which helps prevent overfitting by adding a penalty on the size of the weights.

- `apply_dropout` demonstrates the dropout regularization method, which stochastically drops units from the neural network during training to prevent co-adaptation and improve generalization.

- `augment_data` function provides a framework for applying a pipeline of augmentation transformations to the data, increasing dataset diversity to help model robustness and generalization.

The presented code allows for practical applications and demonstrations of the regularization techniques described theoretically in this chapter. Each function highlights a unique approach to mitigating overfitting and enhancing the learning capability of neural networks.

Chapter 8

Information Bottleneck Theory

Introduction to Information Bottleneck

The Information Bottleneck (IB) theory, a framework initially developed in the context of statistical and information theory, provides a powerful lens through which to examine the role of information flow in neural networks. At its core, the IB principle offers a method for extracting relevant information that a random variable X holds about another random variable Y through a compressed representation T.

The fundamental elements of IB theory seek to minimize the mutual information $I(X;T)$, while maximizing $I(T;Y)$. The principle is mathematically formalized as the optimization problem:

$$\min_{p(t|x)} I(X;T) - \beta I(T;Y)$$

where β is a Lagrange multiplier balancing compression and preservation of information. This trade-off governs the extraction of pertinent information, optimizing the channel through which information flows from inputs to outputs within a neural network.

Theoretical Foundations

In neural network architectures, the IB framework translates to understanding not only the information a network retains but also what it discards. A key intuition of IB theory is that during training, neural networks implicitly compress input representations through architecture bottlenecks, naturally aligning with IB objectives.

Consider the reduction of mutual information $I(X;T)$, which forces the internals of a neural network to only retain information essential to predicting outputs Y. The IB method-involved variational bounds are often utilized to compute an approximation of the optimal representations. These bounds are described by:

$$\mathcal{L}_{IB}(\theta) = -\frac{1}{N} \sum_{n=1}^{N} \left[\mathbb{E}_{p(t|x_n)} \log q(y_n|t) - \beta \cdot KL[p(t|x_n)\|r(t)] \right]$$

where θ represents the model parameters, $q(y_n|t)$ is the likelihood of Y given representation T, and KL denotes the Kullback-Leibler divergence between distributions.

Impact on Learning with Neural Networks

The application of IB principles in deep learning posits that the layers of neural networks can be viewed as a sequence of information-theoretic transformations undergoing compression and relevance learning. A pivotal outcome of this is the layer-wise disentanglement of information, often observed empirically through probing such architectures with IB-based analysis.

Training dynamics within the IB framework suggest that early stages are predominantly focused on fitting training data, while later stages prioritize the compression of input representations, refining the network's ability to generalize by distilling essential features.

1   Generalization and Compression

The notion of simplicity bias inherent in IB theory is instrumental in explaining the generalization capabilities of neural networks. This bias towards simpler representations aligns with structural risk minimization by asserting that over-complex models are implicitly penalized, thereby facilitating robust generalization.

Formally, this relationship ties to how the generalization error $\mathcal{E}_{gen}$ is impacted by compression, as lower mutual information $I(X;T)$ reflects reduced model complexity.

Applications in Modern Architectures

The incorporation of IB principles into the design of neural networks enhances architecture uniformity and redundancy reduction. Techniques such as pruning, dropout, and layer-wise relevance propagation can be conceptually linked to IB's compression concepts.

The construction of architectures with 'bottleneck layers'—layers with reduced dimensionality—demonstrates the applicability of IB principles. These bottleneck layers serve as forced compression mechanisms compelling networks to encode only the most relevant features, thereby fortifying model interpretability and efficiency.

1   Empirical Studies

Recent empirical studies validate the predictive performance improvements stemming from explicitly enforcing IB objectives during training. Incorporating noise and ablation tests that probe resilience and robustness of exchanged representations deepens understanding of how networks can be taught to ignore irrelevancies, preserving information pathways critical to decision-making processes.

Neural Capacity and Information Flow

The nuances of neural capacity explain the limitations and facilitative powers of neural architectures under IB theory. Capacity refers to the network's ability to store and manage information. Proper utilization of this capacity ensures that the essential information aligns across layers to effectively transmit and transform data representations.

IB-driven pruning mechanisms actively manage neural capacity by strategically simplifying network components without substantial loss of accuracy, resulting in optimized flow of pertinent information from input to output.

1   Concluding Remarks on Information Flow

The seamless integration of the Information Bottleneck principle into neural network theory forges profound innovation in understanding and optimizing data representations. Through careful balancing of information retention and minimization, networks are empowered both to learn efficiently and to generalize proficiently, advancing the frontier of machine learning.

Python Code Snippet

Below is a Python code snippet that calculates the core concepts of the Information Bottleneck theory, focusing on mutual information optimization, variational bounds, and the impact of these concepts on neural networks.

```python
import numpy as np
from scipy.stats import entropy

def mutual_information(X, T):
    '''
    Calculate the mutual information between variables X and T.
    :param X: Input variable.
    :param T: Compressed representation.
    :return: Mutual information value.
    '''
    p_x = np.histogram(X, bins=10, density=True)[0]
    p_t = np.histogram(T, bins=10, density=True)[0]
    p_xt = np.histogram2d(X, T, bins=10, density=True)[0]
    return entropy(p_x) + entropy(p_t) - entropy(p_xt)

def information_bottleneck(X, Y, beta, iterations=100):
    '''
    Optimize the IB objective for given variables and beta.
    :param X: Input variable.
    :param Y: Output variable.
    :param beta: Trade-off parameter.
    :param iterations: Number of iterations.
    :return: Optimal representation T and mutual information values.
    '''
    # Initialize T with random values
    T = np.random.rand(len(X))
    I_XT_history, I_TY_history = [], []

    for _ in range(iterations):
        # Estimate mutual information
        I_XT = mutual_information(X, T)
        I_TY = mutual_information(T, Y)

        # Update T according to IB objective
        T -= 0.01 * (I_XT - beta * I_TY)

        # Store history
        I_XT_history.append(I_XT)
        I_TY_history.append(I_TY)
```

```
        return T, I_XT_history, I_TY_history

def neural_network_compression(X, Y, beta):
    '''
    Simulates IB principle on neural network layers.
    :param X: Input data.
    :param Y: Target labels.
    :param beta: Trade-off parameter.
    :return: Compressed representation.
    '''
    # Placeholder activation for a bottleneck layer
    def bottleneck_layer(x):
        return np.tanh(x)

    # Forward pass through a single layer with IB principle applied
    T = bottleneck_layer(X)
    optimal_T, _, _ = information_bottleneck(X, Y, beta)

    return optimal_T

# Example data
X = np.random.rand(1000)
Y = X + np.random.normal(0, 0.1, 1000)  # some function of X with
↪  noise
beta = 0.5

# Optimize IB objective
T, I_XT_history, I_TY_history = information_bottleneck(X, Y, beta)
compressed_representation = neural_network_compression(X, Y, beta)

# Example outputs
print("Optimized Representation:", T[:5])
print("Compressed Representation:", compressed_representation[:5])
print("Mutual Information I(X;T) History:", I_XT_history[:5])
print("Mutual Information I(T;Y) History:", I_TY_history[:5])
```

This code snippet outlines essential functions related to the Information Bottleneck concept in neural networks:

- `mutual_information` calculates the mutual information between input and compressed representations.

- `information_bottleneck` optimizes the Information Bottleneck objective to derive an optimal compressed representation.

- `neural_network_compression` showcases the application of the IB principle within a neural network layer, simulating how data would be compressed in practice.

The provided output serves as examples to illustrate the functioning and result of optimizing the Information Bottleneck with synthetic data.

Chapter 9

Stochasticity in Neural Network Training

Introduction to Stochastic Methods

In the landscape of neural network training, stochastic methods play an integral role in shaping the dynamics of learning processes. Particularly, stochastic gradient descent (SGD) and noise injection techniques are seminal in enhancing the performance and robustness of neural networks by exploiting randomness. Stochasticity, while introducing inherent uncertainty, alleviates several challenges that deterministic approaches face, notably in overcoming local minima and fostering superior generalization capabilities.

Stochastic Gradient Descent and its Variants

The inherent stochastic nature of mini-batch gradient descent, often referred to as stochastic gradient descent (SGD), provides a probabilistic traversal over the parameter space. In its formalism, SGD updates the model parameters θ at each iteration t using a randomly selected mini-batch B_t from the training set:

$$\theta_{t+1} = \theta_t - \eta \nabla_\theta \mathcal{L}(\theta_t, B_t)$$

where η denotes the learning rate and $\nabla_\theta \mathcal{L}(\theta_t, B_t)$ is the gradient of the loss $\mathcal{L}$ with respect to θ, computed over B_t.

SGD inherently incorporates stochasticity by virtue of its mini-batch selection, which aids in escaping from sharp local minima that may trap deterministic optimizers. This characteristic is crucial for neural networks' efficacy, particularly given their highly non-convex loss landscapes.

1 Momentum and Adaptive Methods

In refining the foundational SGD, techniques such as momentum and adaptive learning rate methods, including Adam and RMSprop, introduce nuanced layers of complexity. The momentum update modifies SGD as follows:

$$v_t = \gamma v_{t-1} + \eta \nabla_\theta \mathcal{L}(\theta_t, B_t)$$

$$\theta_{t+1} = \theta_t - v_t$$

where γ is the momentum term. The introduction of v_t facilitates smoother convergence by accumulating past gradients, thus maintaining directional persistence.

These stochastic optimizers further interpolate randomness with learning dynamics, optimizing the trajectory taken in the hyperspace by balancing exploration and exploitation.

Noise Injection and Regularization

Noise injection into neural network training works as a form of implicit regularization, enhancing the network's robustness and generalization potential. In mathematical terms, noise ϵ can be introduced directly into various components such as weights (θ), activations, or inputs (x):

$$\theta = \theta + \epsilon, \quad \epsilon \sim \mathcal{N}(0, \sigma^2)$$

where σ^2 is the variance of the Gaussian noise distribution. This stochastic perturbation compels networks to learn noise-resistant features, enhancing the model's robustness against overfitting and promoting better generalization across unseen data domains.

1 Random Initialization and its Effects

The randomness in initial weight settings is another realm where stochasticity profoundly affects neural network training. Initializing weights using methods like Glorot or He initialization introduces randomness that can decisively impact convergence speed and model performance. Random initialization avoids symmetry in parameter updates, granting diversified paths across the optimization landscape.

Theoretical Impacts on Generalization

Stochastic processes in neural network training are fundamentally tied to the theory of generalization, encapsulated by how models extrapolate learned patterns to unencountered instances. The stochastic exploration of the parameter space often drives towards flatter minima, believed to correlate positively with generalization performance. Broad observations and analyses suggest that flatter loss basins, which SGD tends to locate, exhibit reduced sensitivity to perturbations in input data, a signifier of robust generalization.

Escaping Local Minima

The ability to escape local minima, a noteworthy challenge in training deep neural networks, is significantly bolstered by stochastic methods. These methodologies interfere with deterministic descent, allowing neural networks to circumvent non-prominent optima through probabilistic perturbations in the training trajectory.

Noise and randomness, quintessential components of stochasticity, facilitate such escapades, thus enhancing the overall training dynamics in high-dimensional parameter spaces.

Insights and Implications in Modern Architectures

In the current sphere of neural network architectures, stochasticity influences the design and function of various structural components. Embedding stochastic elements within dropout mechanisms, noise layers, and batch normalization fortifies the network against overfitting and enriches its capacity to generalize.

Network layers that integrate stochastic attributes cultivate redundancies that contribute to an enriched understanding of data complexities and thereby accommodate diverse dataset transformations effectively.

Conclusion

In summation, stochasticity within neural network training paradigms not only enriches the methodological approach towards optimization but also strengthens the subsequent model efficacy through enhanced generalization and robust traversal of the loss landscape. The intricate dance between determinism and chance delineates a path toward neural network transcendence, maneuvering amidst the treacherous topographical challenges posed by complex data.

Python Code Snippet

Below is a Python code snippet that illustrates the implementation of stochastic gradient descent (SGD), momentum, adaptive methods such as Adam, noise injection, and random initialization, reflecting the computational essence mentioned in this chapter.

```python
import numpy as np

def sgd_update(theta, grad, learning_rate):
    '''
    Perform a stochastic gradient descent update.
    :param theta: Current parameters.
    :param grad: Gradient of the loss with respect to parameters.
    :param learning_rate: Step size for the update.
    :return: Updated parameters.
    '''
    return theta - learning_rate * grad

def momentum_update(theta, grad, v, learning_rate, momentum=0.9):
    '''
    Apply momentum for parameter updates.
    :param theta: Current parameters.
    :param grad: Gradient of the loss with respect to parameters.
    :param v: Previous velocity vector.
    :param learning_rate: Step size.
    :param momentum: Momentum factor (default 0.9).
    :return: Updated parameters and velocity.
    '''
    v_new = momentum * v + learning_rate * grad
    theta_update = theta - v_new
    return theta_update, v_new
```

```python
def adam_update(theta, grad, m, v, t, learning_rate=0.001,
                beta1=0.9, beta2=0.999, epsilon=1e-8):
    '''
    Update parameters using Adam optimization.
    :param theta: Current parameters.
    :param grad: Gradient of the loss.
    :param m: First moment vector.
    :param v: Second moment vector.
    :param t: Time step (iteration counter).
    :param learning_rate: Step size.
    :return: Updated parameters, first moment, and second moment.
    '''
    m = beta1 * m + (1 - beta1) * grad
    v = beta2 * v + (1 - beta2) * (grad ** 2)
    m_hat = m / (1 - beta1 ** t)
    v_hat = v / (1 - beta2 ** t)
    theta_update = theta - learning_rate * m_hat / (np.sqrt(v_hat) +
    ↪   epsilon)
    return theta_update, m, v

def inject_noise(data, sigma=0.1):
    '''
    Add Gaussian noise to data.
    :param data: Input data.
    :param sigma: Standard deviation of noise (default 0.1).
    :return: Noisy data.
    '''
    noise = np.random.normal(0, sigma, data.shape)
    return data + noise

def random_init(shape, method='He'):
    '''
    Randomly initialize weights.
    :param shape: Shape of the weights matrix/tensor.
    :param method: Initialization method ('Glorot' or 'He').
    :return: Initialized weights.
    '''
    if method == 'Glorot':
        limit = np.sqrt(6 / np.sum(shape))
    elif method == 'He':
        limit = np.sqrt(2 / shape[0])
    return np.random.uniform(-limit, limit, shape)

# Example usage and results presentation
theta = np.array([0.5, 0.3])
grad = np.array([0.1, 0.2])
v = m = np.zeros(theta.shape)

# Stochastic Gradient Descent
theta_sgd = sgd_update(theta, grad, learning_rate=0.01)
# Momentum-based update
theta_mom, v = momentum_update(theta, grad, v, learning_rate=0.01)
# Adam update
```

```
theta_adam, m, v = adam_update(theta, grad, m, v, t=1)

# Data with noise injection
data = np.array([[1.0, 2.0], [3.0, 4.0]])
noisy_data = inject_noise(data)

# Random weight initialization
weights_glorot = random_init((2, 2), method='Glorot')
weights_he = random_init((2, 2), method='He')

# Print results
print("SGD Updated Parameters:", theta_sgd)
print("Momentum Updated Parameters:", theta_mom)
print("Adam Updated Parameters:", theta_adam)
print("Noisy Data:\n", noisy_data)
print("Weights - Glorot Initialization:\n", weights_glorot)
print("Weights - He Initialization:\n", weights_he)
```

This Python code snippet implements key stochastic methodologies and algorithms used in neural network training:

- `sgd_update` computes parameter updates using basic stochastic gradient descent.

- `momentum_update` applies momentum to accelerate updates in the relevant gradient directions.

- `adam_update` provides parameter updates using the Adam optimization method, incorporating adaptive learning rates.

- `inject_noise` introduces Gaussian noise to simulate noise injection strategies akin to implicit regularization.

- `random_init` initializes neural network weights according to specified strategies like Glorot or He initialization.

These computations enable a nuanced approach to optimizing neural network parameters, balancing exploratory updates with exploitative improvements in performance.

Chapter 10

Bayesian Neural Networks and Uncertainty Quantification

Foundational Concepts in Bayesian Inference

Bayesian neural networks (BNNs) fundamentally integrate the principles of Bayesian inference with the flexible capacity of neural networks. This amalgamation facilitates robust uncertainty quantification within neural models by treating the network parameters θ as random variables with defined prior distributions $p(\theta)$. The posterior distribution $p(\theta \mid \mathcal{D})$ is then obtained, conditioned on the dataset $\mathcal{D}$, represented by Bayes' theorem:

$$p(\theta \mid \mathcal{D}) = \frac{p(\mathcal{D} \mid \theta)p(\theta)}{p(\mathcal{D})}$$

where $p(\mathcal{D} \mid \theta)$ is the likelihood and $p(\mathcal{D})$ the marginal likelihood or evidence.

1 Posterior Inference and Challenges

The analytical computation of $p(\theta \mid \mathcal{D})$ often poses significant challenges due to its intractability in closed form, particularly in high-dimensional parameter spaces. The posterior encapsulates all instances observed and further encompasses the epistemic uncertainty, which reflects model confidence regarding the learned parameters. This necessitates the application of stochastic approximations or deterministic approximations to aid inferential tractability.

Uncertainty Estimation in Neural Networks

In Bayesian neural networks, uncertainty estimation is routinely divided into two forms: aleatoric and epistemic uncertainties. Aleatoric uncertainty arises from data inherent noise, while epistemic uncertainty emerges from the model's ignorance about the optimal parameter configurations. Bayesian neural networks are adept at capturing both phenomena through the probabilistic treatment of parameters.

The predictive posterior distribution given a new data point x^* is:

$$p(y^* \mid x^*, \mathcal{D}) = \int p(y^* \mid x^*, \theta) p(\theta \mid \mathcal{D}) \, d\theta$$

Monte Carlo methods, such as sampling from the posterior, are typically employed to obtain empirical estimations of this distribution.

Variational Inference and Approximation Techniques

Variational inference (VI) provides an efficient, approximate method for Bayesian inference in scenarios where exact solutions are intractable. This approach involves positing a tractable family of distributions $q(\theta)$, then optimizing over these distributions to closely approximate the true posterior.

The approximation objective is typically framed as minimizing the Kullback-Leibler divergence D_{KL} between $q(\theta)$ and $p(\theta \mid \mathcal{D})$:

$$D_{\mathrm{KL}}(q(\theta) \parallel p(\theta \mid \mathcal{D})) = \int q(\theta) \log \frac{q(\theta)}{p(\theta \mid \mathcal{D})} \, d\theta \approx \mathrm{argmin}_q \mathcal{L}(q)$$

where the $\mathcal{L}(q)$ represents the evidence lower bound (ELBO), expressed as:

$$\mathcal{L}(q) = \mathbb{E}_{q(\theta)}[\log p(\mathcal{D} \mid \theta)] - D_{\mathrm{KL}}(q(\theta) \parallel p(\theta))$$

Training Bayesian Neural Networks

Training methods for BNNs often employ stochastic gradient-based approaches adapted for the variational context. The utilization of reparameterization tricks, such as the pathwise derivative method, facilitates gradient-based optimization by converting expectations involving distributions into differentiable forms.

During training, parameter updates are driven by approximating the gradients of the ELBO with respect to the variational parameters, commonly applying:

$$\nabla \mathcal{L}(q) \approx \text{Variance Reduction Techniques}$$

These procedures produce better estimation of uncertainty metrics, such as credible intervals for predictions and the expected mean and variance.

Applications and Implications of Uncertainty Quantification

The estimation of uncertainty has profound implications across numerous machine learning applications. By leveraging BNNs, practitioners can derive predictive distributions rather than point estimates, which vastly enriches decision-making processes where risk assessment and confidence quantification are critical. Moreover, BNNs contribute significantly to active learning by prioritizing data acquisition processes that reduce uncertainty.

Bayesian methodologies supplement deep learning with the critical ability to model and convey inherent uncertainties, thereby advancing robust and interpretable model development.

Python Code Snippet

Below is a Python code snippet that encompasses the core computational elements of Bayesian neural networks, including posterior inference, uncertainty estimation, variational inference, and training procedures.

```python
import torch
import torch.nn as nn
import torch.optim as optim
from torch.distributions import Normal

class BayesianLinear(nn.Module):
    def __init__(self, in_features, out_features):
        super(BayesianLinear, self).__init__()
        self.mu_w = nn.Parameter(torch.Tensor(out_features,
        ↪  in_features).uniform_(-0.2, 0.2))
        self.rho_w = nn.Parameter(torch.Tensor(out_features,
        ↪  in_features).uniform_(-5, -4))
        self.mu_b =
        ↪  nn.Parameter(torch.Tensor(out_features).uniform_(-0.2,
        ↪  0.2))
        self.rho_b =
        ↪  nn.Parameter(torch.Tensor(out_features).uniform_(-5,
        ↪  -4))
        self.sigma_w = torch.log1p(torch.exp(self.rho_w))
        self.sigma_b = torch.log1p(torch.exp(self.rho_b))

    def forward(self, x):
        epsilon_w = Normal(0, 1).sample(self.mu_w.size())
        epsilon_b = Normal(0, 1).sample(self.mu_b.size())
        weights = self.mu_w + self.sigma_w * epsilon_w
        biases = self.mu_b + self.sigma_b * epsilon_b
        return nn.functional.linear(x, weights, biases)

class BayesianNeuralNetwork(nn.Module):
    def __init__(self):
        super(BayesianNeuralNetwork, self).__init__()
        self.layer1 = BayesianLinear(1, 10)
        self.layer2 = BayesianLinear(10, 1)

    def forward(self, x):
        x = torch.relu(self.layer1(x))
        x = self.layer2(x)
        return x

def kl_divergence(mu_q, sigma_q, mu_p=0, sigma_p=1):
    return torch.log(sigma_p / sigma_q) + (sigma_q ** 2 + (mu_q -
    ↪  mu_p) ** 2) / (2 * sigma_p ** 2) - 0.5

def elbo(output, target, kl_lambda):
```

```
likelihood = -torch.nn.functional.mse_loss(output, target,
    reduction='sum')
kl = 0
for module in model.modules():
    if isinstance(module, BayesianLinear):
        kl += kl_divergence(module.mu_w, module.sigma_w).sum()
        kl += kl_divergence(module.mu_b, module.sigma_b).sum()
return likelihood - kl * kl_lambda

def train_bayesian_nn(model, data, targets, epochs=1000, lr=1e-3):
    optimizer = optim.Adam(model.parameters(), lr=lr)
    for epoch in range(epochs):
        model.train()
        optimizer.zero_grad()
        output = model(data)
        loss = -elbo(output, targets, kl_lambda=0.01)
        loss.backward()
        optimizer.step()
        if epoch % 100 == 0:
            print(f'Epoch {epoch} - Loss: {loss.item()}')

# Example usage
model = BayesianNeuralNetwork()
data = torch.Tensor([[1], [2], [3], [4], [5]])
targets = torch.Tensor([[2.2], [2.8], [3.6], [4.0], [5.2]])
train_bayesian_nn(model, data, targets)
```

This code defines several key functions necessary for implementing and training Bayesian neural networks:

- **BayesianLinear** Custom layer for modeling Bayesian linear transformations with learnable parameters as distributions.

- **BayesianNeuralNetwork** A neural network comprising two Bayesian linear layers.

- **kl_divergence** Calculates the Kullback-Leibler divergence used in variational approximation.

- **elbo** Computes the evidence lower bound (ELBO), balancing likelihood and complexity.

- **train_bayesian_nn** Trains the Bayesian neural network via stochastic optimization, minimizing the ELBO.

The final block of code provides an example of training the Bayesian neural network with dummy data.

66

Chapter 11

Neural Networks as Dynamical Systems

Neural Networks and Dynamical Systems Theory

Neural networks can be effectively modeled as dynamical systems, where their training processes mirror evolving systems governed by specific mathematical formulations. A neural network can be represented as a state vector, $\mathbf{x}(t)$, evolving over time t according to a dynamic rule. In discrete time, this evolution can be written as:

$$\mathbf{x}(t+1) = F(\mathbf{x}(t), \mathbf{w}(t))$$

where F represents the transformation function defined by the network, with parameters $\mathbf{w}(t)$ subject to learning dynamics.

Stability Analysis of Neural Networks

The stability of a neural network as a dynamical system determines its ability to converge to a fixed point or desired trajectory. Such analysis often involves examining the equilibria of the system, derived from the condition:

$$\mathbf{x}^* = F(\mathbf{x}^*, \mathbf{w})$$

Linear stability analysis requires linearizing the system around an equilibrium point $\mathbf{x}^*$. This process involves calculating the Jacobian matrix $\mathbf{J}$ at $\mathbf{x}^*$:

$$\mathbf{J} = \left.\frac{\partial F}{\partial \mathbf{x}}\right|_{\mathbf{x}=\mathbf{x}^*}$$

The eigenvalues of $\mathbf{J}$ determine the stability of the equilibrium. If all eigenvalues have magnitudes less than one, the system is locally stable at $\mathbf{x}^*$.

Training Dynamics and Fixed Points

Training dynamics of neural networks involve the iterative update of parameters within a high-dimensional space. Viewing training as a dynamical system offers insights into the existence of fixed points, their role in convergence, and learning trajectories. The update rule, often guided by gradient descent, is:

$$\mathbf{w}(t+1) = \mathbf{w}(t) - \eta \nabla_{\mathbf{w}} L(\mathbf{x}(t), \mathbf{w}(t))$$

where L is the loss function and η the learning rate.

In this context, a fixed point is a parameter setting $\mathbf{w}^*$ where:

$$\nabla_{\mathbf{w}} L(\mathbf{x}(t), \mathbf{w}^*) = 0$$

Indicating local minima or saddle points. The characteristic spectrum of such fixed points impacts training success and convergence rates.

Role of Nonlinearity and Chaos

Nonlinearity arising from activation functions such as 'relu', 'tanh', or 'sigmoid' introduces complex dynamics, potentially leading to chaotic behavior. Such behavior complicates the understanding of network convergence. The Lyapunov exponent λ characterizes the sensitivity to initial conditions:

$$\lim_{t \to \infty} \frac{1}{t} \ln |\delta \mathbf{x}(t)| = \lambda$$

A positive Lyapunov exponent $\lambda > 0$ suggests chaotic dynamics, posing a significant challenge to stable convergence.

Attractors in Neural Network Training

The concept of attractors in dynamical systems is crucial to understanding the behavior of neural networks during training. An attractor is a set of states toward which a system tends to evolve. In neural networks, these are configurations in parameter space where training terminates or oscillates. The attractor basin's structure influences the network's robustness:

$$B(\mathbf{x}^*) = \{\mathbf{x}(0) \mid \lim_{t \to \infty} \mathbf{x}(t) = \mathbf{x}^*\}$$

Understanding attractor basins enables the exploration of network generalization across varying initializations.

Empirical Evidence and Implication on Practice

Empirical studies support the theory of neural networks as dynamical systems, showcasing how their optimization landscapes mirror dynamical phenomena. Such insights guide model architecture design, regularization techniques, and the selection of optimization strategies distinctively tuned to the networks' learned dynamical properties, as illustrated by the landscape's topography and the energy levels associated with different parameter configurations.

By drawing parallels between neural network training and dynamical systems, theoretical studies inform practical approaches towards deploying more robust and efficient learning algorithms.

Python Code Snippet

Below is a Python code snippet that implements core computational elements related to modeling neural networks as dynamical systems, including stability analysis, training dynamics, and the role of nonlinearity and chaos.

```python
import numpy as np

def dynamic_evolution(x_t, w_t, F):
    '''
    Compute the next state of the system given the current state and
    ↪    parameters.
```

```
        :param x_t: Current state vector.
        :param w_t: Current parameter vector.
        :param F: Transformation function.
        :return: Next state vector.
        '''
        return F(x_t, w_t)

    def stability_analysis(F, x_star, w):
        '''
        Perform linear stability analysis of the neural network as a
        ↪  dynamical system.
        :param F: Transformation function.
        :param x_star: Equilibrium point.
        :param w: Parameter vector.
        :return: Eigenvalues of the Jacobian.
        '''
        J = np.array([[F(i, w_partial) for w_partial in w] for i in
        ↪  x_star])
        # Compute the eigenvalues of the Jacobian matrix
        eigenvalues = np.linalg.eigvals(J)
        return eigenvalues

    def gradient_descent_step(w_t, x_t, L, eta):
        '''
        Perform a single gradient descent step.
        :param w_t: Current parameter vector.
        :param x_t: Current state vector.
        :param L: Loss function.
        :param eta: Learning rate.
        :return: Updated parameter vector.
        '''
        gradient = np.gradient(L(x_t, w_t))
        w_t_next = w_t - eta * gradient
        return w_t_next

    def find_fixed_points(L, x, w):
        '''
        Identify fixed points in training dynamics.
        :param L: Loss function.
        :param x: Current state vector.
        :param w: Parameter vector.
        :return: Fixed points as a list of parameter settings.
        '''
        gradient = np.gradient(L(x, w))
        fixed_points = np.where(np.isclose(gradient, 0))
        return fixed_points

    def lyapunov_exponent(delta_x, t):
        '''
        Calculate the Lyapunov exponent indicating chaotic behavior.
        :param delta_x: Change in state over time.
        :param t: Time vector.
        :return: Lyapunov exponent.
```

```python
    ''' 
    return (1 / t) * np.log(np.abs(delta_x))

def attractor_basins(x_star, x0):
    '''
    Construct the basin of attraction for a given equilibrium point.
    :param x_star: Equilibrium point.
    :param x0: Initial state.
    :return: Basin of attraction.
    '''
    basin = {tuple(x) for x in x0 if
        ↪ np.all(np.isclose(dynamic_evolution(x, None, F), x_star))}
    return basin

# Example values and constants
F = lambda x, w: np.tanh(x + w)
x_t = np.array([0.5, 1.0])
w_t = np.array([0.2, 0.3])
eta = 0.01

# Performing a single gradient descent update
L = lambda x, w: np.sum((x - w) ** 2)    # Example loss function
new_w = gradient_descent_step(w_t, x_t, L, eta)
print("Updated Parameters after Gradient Descent:", new_w)

# Analyze stability at a point
x_star = np.array([1.0, 2.0])
eigenvalues = stability_analysis(F, x_star, w_t)
print("Eigenvalues for Stability Analysis:", eigenvalues)

# Calculate Lyapunov exponent
delta_x = np.array([0.01, 0.02])    # Small perturbation
time_vector = np.array([1, 2, 3, 4, 5])
lyapunov = lyapunov_exponent(delta_x, time_vector)
print("Lyapunov Exponent:", lyapunov)

# Determine attractor basins
initial_points = np.random.rand(10, 2)
basins = attractor_basins(x_star, initial_points)
print("Attractor Basins:", basins)
```

This code defines several key functions necessary for the implementation and analysis of neural networks as dynamical systems:

- `dynamic_evolution` function computes the next state vector using a transformation function, simulating neural network dynamics.

- `stability_analysis` performs linear stability analysis, identifying eigenvalues that indicate stability properties around given equilibria.

71

- `gradient_descent_step` updates the parameter vector using a basic gradient descent step, helpful in understanding training as dynamical evolution.

- `find_fixed_points` identifies potential fixed points where the gradient of the loss function equals zero.

- `lyapunov_exponent` calculates the Lyapunov exponent as a measure of chaos or system sensitivity to initial conditions.

- `attractor_basins` identifies basins of attraction around equilibrium points, elucidating convergence areas during training.

The provided code illustrates practical approaches to employing dynamical systems theory in analyzing neural networks, offering insights into their training stability and convergence behavior.

Chapter 12

Representation Learning and Feature Space Geometry

The Art of Representation Learning

Representation learning, central to neural network success, involves the discovery of meaningful data representations. These representations are often formed hierarchically in deep neural networks, enabling complex features to be distilled from raw input data. This hierarchy is constructed through successive layers, each performing a series of transformations. The transformation function applied at layer l, parameterized by weights $\mathbf{W}^{(l)}$ and bias $\mathbf{b}^{(l)}$, is represented by:

$$\mathbf{h}^{(l)} = f(\mathbf{W}^{(l)}\mathbf{h}^{(l-1)} + \mathbf{b}^{(l)})$$

where f is the non-linear activation function, typically chosen from sigmoid, tanh, or rectified linear units (ReLU).

Feature Space Geometry

Deep networks project data into a latent feature space, whose geometry fundamentally influences learning efficacy and generalization. Central to this space is the concept of manifolds, low-dimensional structures embedded within the higher-dimensional input space. Through training, neural networks learn to map input data onto or near these manifolds that capture the intrinsic data properties.

Consider a data point $\mathbf{x}$ mapped to a feature space by a transformation ϕ:

$$\phi(\mathbf{x}) \in \mathcal{M}, \quad \mathcal{M} \subset \mathbb{R}^d$$

where $\mathcal{M}$ denotes the learned manifold. The network's ability to disentangle data points along $\mathcal{M}$ often determines the robustness of learned representations, making it an area of intense theoretical study.

Gradient Flow and Representation Disentanglement

During training, the flow of gradients through a network influences how data representations are shaped. Let L denote a general loss function minimized over network weights during training:

$$\min_{\mathbf{W}} \; L(\hat{\mathbf{y}}, \phi(\mathbf{x}))$$

where $\hat{\mathbf{y}}$ is the predicted output. The differential structure of ϕ determines the optimization trajectory within the feature space, affecting how manifold structures are navigated and representations disentangled.

Given local coordinates $\mathbf{z}$ of $\mathcal{M}$, the tangent space at point $\phi(\mathbf{x})$ can be expressed using the Jacobian matrix $\mathbf{J} = \frac{\partial \phi}{\partial \mathbf{x}}$. For representation disentanglement:

$$\mathbf{J}^T \mathbf{J} \approx \mathbf{I}$$

ensures orthogonality of tangential components, facilitating improved separability of features within $\mathcal{M}$.

Metrics in Feature Spaces

The metric space structure of feature representations provides a quantitative assessment of similarity and distance between data points. Neural architecture dictates the metric tensor g, intrinsic to the feature space:

74

$$g_{ij} = \frac{\partial \phi_i}{\partial \mathbf{x}} \cdot \frac{\partial \phi_j}{\partial \mathbf{x}}$$

The choice of g impacts the notion of distance $\mathbf{d}$ in the feature space, influencing the network's ability to generalize across tasks and domains:

$$\mathbf{d}(\phi(\mathbf{x}_1), \phi(\mathbf{x}_2)) = \sqrt{(\phi(\mathbf{x}_1) - \phi(\mathbf{x}_2))^T g(\phi(\mathbf{x}_1) - \phi(\mathbf{x}_2))}$$

Implications for Transfer Learning

The efficacy of transfer learning is predicated on the ability to leverage pre-learned feature representations across different but related tasks. A well-generalized representation space is characterized by its adaptability, encoded through shared intrinsic geometric structures.

For a source task $\mathcal{T}_s$ and a target task $\mathcal{T}_t$, the transferability measure $\mathcal{T}$ is often reflected in parameter initialization and adaptation through fine-tuning:

$$\mathcal{T}(\phi_s(\mathbf{x}), \phi_t(\mathbf{x})) = \int_{\mathcal{M}_s \cap \mathcal{M}_t} e^{-||\phi_s(\mathbf{x}) - \phi_t(\mathbf{x})||} \, d\mathbf{x}$$

Continuing research into feature space geometries endeavors to bridge domain gaps, refining transfer learning methodologies.

Python Code Snippet

Below is a Python code snippet that encapsulates the essential computational elements related to representation learning and feature space geometry, including mapping data to feature spaces, disentangling representations, and incorporating transfer learning measures.

```
import numpy as np

def nonlinear_transformation(W, b, h_prev, activation_func):
    '''
    Applies a nonlinear transformation to layer outputs.
    :param W: Weights matrix of the current layer.
    :param b: Bias vector of the current layer.
    :param h_prev: Output from the previous layer.
```

```
    :param activation_func: Activation function to apply.
    :return: Transformed output.
    '''
    z = np.dot(W, h_prev) + b
    return activation_func(z)

def sigmoid(x):
    return 1 / (1 + np.exp(-x))

def relu(x):
    return np.maximum(0, x)

def transform_to_feature_space(x, phi_function):
    '''
    Maps input data points to a latent feature space.
    :param x: Input data point.
    :param phi_function: Transformation function mapping to the
    ↪    feature space.
    :return: Feature space representation of the input.
    '''
    return phi_function(x)

def calculate_jacobian(phi, x):
    '''
    Computes the Jacobian matrix of transformation phi at point x.
    :param phi: Transformation function.
    :param x: Input data point.
    :return: Jacobian matrix.
    '''
    eps = 1e-5
    n = x.shape[0]
    J = np.zeros((n, n))
    for i in range(n):
        perturbed_x = np.copy(x)
        perturbed_x[i] += eps
        J[:, i] = (phi(perturbed_x) - phi(x)) / eps
    return J

def calculate_metric_tensor(J):
    '''
    Computes the metric tensor from the Jacobian matrix.
    :param J: Jacobian matrix.
    :return: Metric tensor.
    '''
    return np.dot(J.T, J)

def compute_transferability(phi_s, phi_t, x_values):
    '''
    Evaluates the transferability measure between source and target
    ↪    task feature spaces.
    :param phi_s: Feature space mapping for the source task.
    :param phi_t: Feature space mapping for the target task.
    :param x_values: Data points for integration.
```

```
    :return: Transferability metric.
    '''
    transferability = 0
    for x in x_values:
        diff = phi_s(x) - phi_t(x)
        transferability += np.exp(-np.linalg.norm(diff))
    return transferability / len(x_values)

# Example transformations
W = np.array([[0.5, -0.2], [0.1, 0.4]])
b = np.array([0.1, 0.2])
h_prev = np.array([0.3, 0.5])
phi = lambda x: np.dot(W, x) + b

# Feature space transformation example
feature_representation = transform_to_feature_space(h_prev, phi)
Jacobian_matrix = calculate_jacobian(phi, h_prev)
metric_tensor = calculate_metric_tensor(Jacobian_matrix)

# Transfer learning elements
phi_source = lambda x: x * 0.8
phi_target = lambda x: x * 1.1
x_samples = [np.array([1.0, 2.0]), np.array([2.5, 3.0]),
↪   np.array([3.5, 4.0])]
transferability_metric = compute_transferability(phi_source,
↪   phi_target, x_samples)

# Demonstration output
print("Feature Space Representation:", feature_representation)
print("Jacobian Matrix:\n", Jacobian_matrix)
print("Metric Tensor:\n", metric_tensor)
print("Transferability Metric:", transferability_metric)
```

This code covers several critical aspects of representation learning and analyses of feature space geometries:

- `nonlinear_transformation` applies a transformation to extract features using learned weights and biases with an activation function.

- `transform_to_feature_space` maps inputs into the feature space using a specified transformation function.

- `calculate_jacobian` computes the Jacobian matrix at a point in the feature space for local coordinate transformations.

- `calculate_metric_tensor` derives the metric tensor from the Jacobian, influencing geometry in the feature space.

- `compute_transferability` assesses how well learned features can be transferred between related tasks or domains.

The provided code snippet demonstrates these computations with example parameters and transformation functions, illustrating how neural networks manage feature space transformations and adapt representations for transfer learning.

Chapter 13

Theoretical Insights into Convolutional Neural Networks

Translational Invariance in CNNs

Convolutional Neural Networks (CNNs) leverage translational invariance as a core architectural principle, enabling robust feature detection irrespective of spatial position. This invariance is achieved through the convolution operation, defined for an input image $\mathbf{X}$ and a filter $\mathbf{K}$ as:

$$(\mathbf{X} * \mathbf{K})(i, j) = \sum_m \sum_n \mathbf{X}(i + m, j + n) \cdot \mathbf{K}(m, n)$$

By applying weight-sharing mechanisms, CNNs ensure the learned filters are location agnostic, responding equally to patterns regardless of their position in the visual field. The translation of a feature within an image typically results in a corresponding translation of its response in the feature map, preserving the spatial hierarchy without requiring explicit re-calibration throughout the learning process.

Receptive Fields and Hierarchical Feature Extraction

The receptive field of a neuron within a CNN refers to the region of the input space that influences that neuron's activation. Each subsequent convolutional layer in a CNN effectively extends the receptive field, aggregating local information into more global context. Formally, for a given layer l, the effective receptive field R_l can be recursively defined as:

$$R_l = (R_{l-1} - 1) \cdot S_l + K_l$$

where S_l is the stride and K_l is the kernel size of the filter. As l increases, the network captures more complex and abstract representations, allowing the deeper layers to form global perceptions of objects by integrating information across extended input regions.

Theoretical Justifications for Layered Architectures

The design of layered architectures in CNNs is rooted in their capacity to approximate complex functions. The foundational theoretical underpinning stems from the universal approximation theorem, which states that a feedforward network with a single hidden layer containing a finite number of neurons can approximate any continuous function. In the context of CNNs, multiple layers are employed not merely for function approximation, but for enhanced feature construction and hierarchical learning.

The function approximation power of a CNN can be quantified by the concept of depth and width. Depth refers to the number of layers, and width refers to the number of units in each layer. Function f encoded by a CNN is:

$$f(\mathbf{x}) = \sigma \left(W^{(L)} \cdot \sigma \left(W^{(L-1)} \cdots \sigma(W^{(1)}\mathbf{x} + b^{(1)}) \cdots + b^{(L-1)} \right) + b^{(L)} \right)$$

where σ is a non-linear activation function like ReLU. The depth contributes to the expressiveness by enabling the transformation and composition of simple motifs into complex structures. Shallow networks, while potentially wide enough, would require exponentially larger parameters to achieve equivalent expressive power.

Architectural Choices: Stride, Padding, and Pooling

The nuances of CNN architectural design involve selecting appropriate parameters such as stride, padding, and pooling. These components drastically modulate the sensitivity and efficiency of a network. The stride S influences the spatial resolution of feature maps by skipping a fixed number of pixels, effectively down-sampling the input, modeled as:

$$O = \left\lfloor \frac{I - K + 2P}{S} \right\rfloor + 1$$

where O is the output dimension, I is the input dimension, K is the filter size, and P is the padding. Padding impacts the preservation of spatial dimensions, commonly applied as 'same' or 'valid'. Additionally, pooling layers, often max-pooling, serve to reduce dimensionality and computational overhead, defined mathematically for a pooling region R as:

$$\max_{\mathbf{x} \in R} \mathbf{x}$$

Pooling introduces a form of spatial invariance, aiding the model in maintaining the trajectory of significant features while ignoring minute variations.

In ensemble, these architectural insights harness mathematical properties to formulate efficient and generalizable CNNs, supporting the extraction and amalgamation of multi-scale, nuanced features from raw data inputs.

Python Code Snippet

Below is a Python code snippet implementing key computational aspects of Convolutional Neural Networks (CNNs) related to translational invariance, receptive fields, layered architectures, and architectural parameters such as stride, padding, and pooling.

```python
import numpy as np

def convolve_2d(image, kernel, stride, padding):
    '''
    Performs 2D convolution on an image.
```

```
    :param image: Input image matrix.
    :param kernel: Filter matrix.
    :param stride: Stride value for the convolution.
    :param padding: Padding value for the convolution.
    :return: Convolved image.
    '''
    img_height, img_width = image.shape
    kernel_height, kernel_width = kernel.shape

    # Add zero-padding to the input image
    image_padded = np.pad(image, [(padding, padding), (padding,
    ↪    padding)], mode='constant', constant_values=0)

    # Calculate output dimensions
    output_height = (img_height - kernel_height + 2 * padding) //
    ↪    stride + 1
    output_width = (img_width - kernel_width + 2 * padding) //
    ↪    stride + 1

    # Initialize the output
    output = np.zeros((output_height, output_width))

    # Perform the convolution
    for i in range(output_height):
        for j in range(output_width):
            vert_start = i * stride
            vert_end = vert_start + kernel_height
            horiz_start = j * stride
            horiz_end = horiz_start + kernel_width

            output[i, j] = np.sum(kernel *
            ↪    image_padded[vert_start:vert_end,
            ↪    horiz_start:horiz_end])

    return output

def calculate_receptive_field(layer_structure):
    '''
    Calculate the receptive field size for each layer in a CNN.
    :param layer_structure: List of tuples representing
    ↪    (kernel_size, stride) for each layer.
    :return: List of receptive field sizes per layer.
    '''
    receptive_field = 1
    for kernel_size, stride in layer_structure:
        receptive_field = (receptive_field - 1) * stride +
        ↪    kernel_size
    return receptive_field

def pooling_layer(pooling_region, pooling_type='max'):
    '''
    Apply pooling operation on pooling regions.
    :param pooling_region: Region to pool from.
```

```python
    :param pooling_type: Type of pooling; 'max' or 'average'.
    :return: Pooling result.
    '''
    if pooling_type == 'max':
        return np.max(pooling_region)
    elif pooling_type == 'average':
        return np.mean(pooling_region)
    else:
        raise ValueError("Unsupported pooling type. Choose 'max' or
        ↪  'average'.")

def initialize_weights_and_biases(layers):
    '''
    Initialize weights and biases for CNN layers.
    :param layers: List of tuples representing (previous_layer_size,
    ↪  current_layer_size).
    :return: List of initialized weights and biases.
    '''
    weights = [np.random.randn(current, prev) for prev, current in
    ↪  layers]
    biases = [np.random.randn(current, 1) for _, current in layers]
    return weights, biases


# Example neural network architecture parameters
architecture_params = [
    (3, 2),   # Layer 1: kernel_size = 3, stride = 2
    (3, 1),   # Layer 2: kernel_size = 3, stride = 1
    (3, 1)    # Layer 3: kernel_size = 3, stride = 1
]

# Initialize example weights and biases
weights, biases = initialize_weights_and_biases([(3, 5), (5, 10),
↪  (10, 2)])

# Example image and kernel for convolution operation
example_image = np.random.rand(8, 8)
example_kernel = np.random.rand(3, 3)

# Applying convolution
conv_result = convolve_2d(example_image, example_kernel, stride=1,
↪  padding=1)

# Calculate receptive field for the entire network
rec_field_size = calculate_receptive_field(architecture_params)

# Print result outputs
print("Convolution Result:\n", conv_result)
print("Receptive Field Size:", rec_field_size)
```

This code encapsulates critical functions utilized in CNN implementations:

- `convolve_2d` performs the 2D convolution operation on an input image using a kernel with given stride and padding.

- `calculate_receptive_field` computes the receptive field size of a CNN layer by layer based on the architecture parameters.

- `pooling_layer` applies a pooling operation, supporting both maximum and average pooling strategies, to a section of feature maps.

- `initialize_weights_and_biases` facilitates the initialization of weights and biases based on layer configurations for a CNN.

The code showcases practical examples of these computations, providing a detailed view into CNN operations and configurations.

Chapter 14

Recurrent Neural Networks and Sequence Modeling

The Structure of Recurrent Neural Networks

Recurrent Neural Networks (RNNs) are designed to model sequential data through cyclical connections, enabling them to maintain a hidden state $\mathbf{h}_t$ that evolves over time. Formally, the hidden state at time t is computed as:

$$\mathbf{h}_t = \phi(\mathbf{W}_{hh}\mathbf{h}_{t-1} + \mathbf{W}_{xh}\mathbf{x}_t + \mathbf{b}_h)$$

where ϕ is an activation function, typically a non-linear function like `tanh` or `ReLU`, $\mathbf{W}_{hh}$ represents the recurrent connection weights, $\mathbf{W}_{xh}$ denotes the input connection weights, $\mathbf{x}_t$ is the input vector at time t, and $\mathbf{b}_h$ is a bias term.

RNNs face the problem of vanishing and exploding gradients during backpropagation through time (BPTT). This stems from the repeated multiplication of gradients by $\mathbf{W}_{hh}$, limiting the memory of RNNs over long sequences.

Long Short-Term Memory Networks

Long Short-Term Memory (LSTM) networks introduce a gating mechanism to overcome the limitations of traditional RNNs in capturing long-range dependencies. The LSTM cell comprises three gates: input gate $\mathbf{i}_t$, forget gate $\mathbf{f}_t$, and output gate $\mathbf{o}_t$. The cell state $\mathbf{c}_t$ is updated as follows:

$$\mathbf{f}_t = \sigma(\mathbf{W}_{xf}\mathbf{x}_t + \mathbf{W}_{hf}\mathbf{h}_{t-1} + \mathbf{b}_f)$$

$$\mathbf{i}_t = \sigma(\mathbf{W}_{xi}\mathbf{x}_t + \mathbf{W}_{hi}\mathbf{h}_{t-1} + \mathbf{b}_i)$$

$$\mathbf{o}_t = \sigma(\mathbf{W}_{xo}\mathbf{x}_t + \mathbf{W}_{ho}\mathbf{h}_{t-1} + \mathbf{b}_o)$$

$$\mathbf{g}_t = \tanh(\mathbf{W}_{xg}\mathbf{x}_t + \mathbf{W}_{hg}\mathbf{h}_{t-1} + \mathbf{b}_g)$$

The cell state is modulated by the input and forget gates:

$$\mathbf{c}_t = \mathbf{f}_t \odot \mathbf{c}_{t-1} + \mathbf{i}_t \odot \mathbf{g}_t$$

The hidden state $\mathbf{h}_t$ is computed as:

$$\mathbf{h}_t = \mathbf{o}_t \odot \tanh(\mathbf{c}_t)$$

The multiplicative gates control the information flow, allowing LSTMs to maintain long-term dependencies effectively.

Gated Recurrent Units

Gated Recurrent Units (GRUs) simplify the LSTM architecture by merging the forget and input gates into an update gate and eliminating the separate cell state. The GRU equations are:

$$\mathbf{z}_t = \sigma(\mathbf{W}_{xz}\mathbf{x}_t + \mathbf{W}_{hz}\mathbf{h}_{t-1} + \mathbf{b}_z)$$

$$\mathbf{r}_t = \sigma(\mathbf{W}_{xr}\mathbf{x}_t + \mathbf{W}_{hr}\mathbf{h}_{t-1} + \mathbf{b}_r)$$

The candidate activation is computed as:

$$\tilde{\mathbf{h}}_t = \tanh(\mathbf{W}_{xh}\mathbf{x}_t + \mathbf{r}_t \odot (\mathbf{W}_{hh}\mathbf{h}_{t-1}) + \mathbf{b}_h)$$

The final hidden state is given by:

$$\mathbf{h}_t = (1 - \mathbf{z}_t) \odot \mathbf{h}_{t-1} + \mathbf{z}_t \odot \tilde{\mathbf{h}}_t$$

GRUs offer a more computationally efficient and streamlined architecture compared to LSTMs, while still managing long-range sequence dynamics.

Temporal Dependencies in Sequence Modeling

Modeling temporal dependencies is critical in a variety of applications such as natural language processing, time-series forecasting, and speech recognition. Both LSTMs and GRUs are designed to address these dependencies through mechanisms that track information flow over time. The fundamental challenge lies in balancing short-term and long-term memory over dynamically changing contexts.

The strength of recurrent architectures is their ability to create fixed-dimensional vector representations of sequences of arbitrary length, capturing both syntactic and semantic information. The recurrent structure allows sequential information to be processed in a manner that accounts for context, where later inputs can be influenced by previously observed data.

In sequence-to-sequence tasks, it is common to employ a pair of RNNs configured as an encoder-decoder architecture. The encoder processes the input sequence to compute a context vector, and the decoder mirrors this process to generate an output sequence. This framework is integral to neural machine translation and other structured sequence tasks.

Python Code Snippet

Below is a Python code snippet that encompasses the core computational elements of Recurrent Neural Networks (RNNs), Long Short-Term Memory (LSTM) networks, and Gated Recurrent Units (GRUs), including their forward-pass calculations.

```python
import numpy as np

def rnn_forward(x_t, h_t_prev, W_hh, W_xh, b_h, activation='tanh'):
    '''Compute the forward pass for a single RNN cell.'''
```

```
        if activation == 'tanh':
            phi = np.tanh
        elif activation == 'relu':
            phi = np.maximum

        h_t = phi(np.dot(W_hh, h_t_prev) + np.dot(W_xh, x_t) + b_h)
        return h_t

def lstm_cell_forward(x_t, h_t_prev, c_t_prev, W_xi, W_hi, b_i,
↪    W_xf, W_hf, b_f,
                        W_xo, W_ho, b_o, W_xg, W_hg, b_g):
        '''Compute the forward pass for a single LSTM cell.'''
        i_t = sigmoid(np.dot(W_xi, x_t) + np.dot(W_hi, h_t_prev) + b_i)
        f_t = sigmoid(np.dot(W_xf, x_t) + np.dot(W_hf, h_t_prev) + b_f)
        o_t = sigmoid(np.dot(W_xo, x_t) + np.dot(W_ho, h_t_prev) + b_o)
        g_t = np.tanh(np.dot(W_xg, x_t) + np.dot(W_hg, h_t_prev) + b_g)

        c_t = f_t * c_t_prev + i_t * g_t
        h_t = o_t * np.tanh(c_t)

        return h_t, c_t

def gru_cell_forward(x_t, h_t_prev, W_xz, W_hz, b_z, W_xr, W_hr,
↪    b_r, W_xh,
                        W_hh, b_h):
        '''Compute the forward pass for a single GRU cell.'''
        z_t = sigmoid(np.dot(W_xz, x_t) + np.dot(W_hz, h_t_prev) + b_z)
        r_t = sigmoid(np.dot(W_xr, x_t) + np.dot(W_hr, h_t_prev) + b_r)

        h_tilde = np.tanh(np.dot(W_xh, x_t) + r_t * np.dot(W_hh,
↪    h_t_prev) + b_h)

        h_t = (1 - z_t) * h_t_prev + z_t * h_tilde

        return h_t

def sigmoid(x):
        '''Sigmoid activation function.'''
        return 1 / (1 + np.exp(-x))

# Example of initializing weights and biases for LSTM
input_size = 3
hidden_size = 4

W_xi = np.random.randn(hidden_size, input_size)
W_hi = np.random.randn(hidden_size, hidden_size)
b_i = np.random.randn(hidden_size)

W_xf = np.random.randn(hidden_size, input_size)
W_hf = np.random.randn(hidden_size, hidden_size)
b_f = np.random.randn(hidden_size)

W_xo = np.random.randn(hidden_size, input_size)
```

```
W_ho = np.random.randn(hidden_size, hidden_size)
b_o = np.random.randn(hidden_size)

W_xg = np.random.randn(hidden_size, input_size)
W_hg = np.random.randn(hidden_size, hidden_size)
b_g = np.random.randn(hidden_size)

# Example input and previous states for LSTM
x_t = np.random.randn(input_size)
h_t_prev = np.random.randn(hidden_size)
c_t_prev = np.random.randn(hidden_size)

# Forward pass for LSTM
h_t, c_t = lstm_cell_forward(x_t, h_t_prev, c_t_prev, W_xi, W_hi,
↪  b_i, W_xf, W_hf, b_f,
                             W_xo, W_ho, b_o, W_xg, W_hg, b_g)

print("LSTM hidden state:", h_t)
print("LSTM cell state:", c_t)
```

This code outlines the essential forward-pass calculations for various recurrent network architectures:

- **rnn_forward** function calculates the hidden state for a classical RNN cell using a specified activation function, enabling sequence modeling through cyclical connections.

- **lstm_cell_forward** provides the core computations for an LSTM cell, integrating input, forget, and output gates with memory cell updates for handling long-range dependencies.

- **gru_cell_forward** simplifies sequence processing by merging gates into an update mechanism, balancing simplicity and power in maintaining relevant data longer.

- **sigmoid** calculates the sigmoid activation, frequently used in gate functions in LSTM and GRU cells.

The final code demonstrates initializing and executing a forward pass of an LSTM network using random data to verify the network architecture's computations.

Chapter 15

Attention Mechanisms and Transformer Architectures

Attention Mechanisms

Attention mechanisms have revolutionized the field of sequence transduction by enabling models to dynamically focus on relevant parts of the input sequence. Formally, an attention mechanism can be expressed as a function mapping a query and a set of key-value pairs to an output, where the query, keys, values, and output are all vectors. The output is computed as a weighted sum of the values, with weights assigned in proportion to a similarity function between the query and keys. The most prevalent form is the scaled dot-product attention, defined as:

$$\text{Attention}(Q, K, V) = \texttt{softmax}\left(\frac{QK^T}{\sqrt{d_k}}\right)V$$

where Q is the query matrix, K is the keys matrix, V is the values matrix, and d_k is the dimension of the keys.

1 Multi-Head Attention

To enhance the model's ability to focus on various parts of the input, multi-head attention is employed, which involves executing several attention mechanisms in parallel and concatenating their results. For each attention head i, the inputs Q, K, V are linearly projected onto queries, keys, and values matrices:

$$\text{head}_i = \text{Attention}(QW_i^Q, KW_i^K, VW_i^V)$$

The multi-head attention is then formed by concatenating all heads and projecting the concatenated output:

$$\text{MultiHead}(Q, K, V) = \texttt{Concat}(\text{head}_1, \dots, \text{head}_h)W^O$$

where W_i^Q, W_i^K, W_i^V, W^O are parameter matrices learned during training, and h denotes the number of heads.

The Transformer Model

The Transformer model architecture, devised for handling sequence-to-sequence tasks while forgoing the need for recurrent operations, leverages self-attention mechanisms for input and output representations. The architecture chiefly consists of an encoder and a decoder, both composed of stacked identical layers.

1 Encoder Architecture

Each encoder layer consists of two primary components: multi-head self-attention and position-wise feed-forward networks. An input sequence first passes through the multi-head self-attention block:

$$\text{SelfAttention}(X) = \text{MultiHead}(X, X, X)$$

Here, the self-attention module operates on the unaltered sequence, permitting the position-wise aggregation of context. Following this, the position-wise feed-forward networks, composed of two linear transformations with a ReLU activation in between, process each position separately and identically:

$$\text{FFN}(x) = \max(0, xW_1 + b_1)W_2 + b_2$$

where W_1, W_2 and b_1, b_2 are learnable parameters.

2 Decoder Architecture

The decoder similarly comprises attention and feed-forward networks with an additional encoder-decoder attention layer to focus on the encoder's output:

$$\text{EncDecAttention}(Y, E) = \text{MultiHead}(YW^Q, EW^K, EW^V)$$

where Y is the decoder input, and E is the encoder output. The decoder's purpose includes generating outputs by attending to relevant encoder-side information.

3 Positional Encoding

Transformers lack the inherent sequence-order processing of RNNs; hence, they utilize positional encodings to inject sequence order. The positional encoding PE for position pos and dimension i is defined as:

$$PE_{(pos,2i)} = \sin\left(\frac{pos}{10000^{2i/d_{model}}}\right)$$

$$PE_{(pos,2i+1)} = \cos\left(\frac{pos}{10000^{2i/d_{model}}}\right)$$

where d_{model} is the model dimensionality. These encodings are added to the input embeddings, enabling the model to capture positional information.

Theoretical Implications

Attention mechanisms and Transformer architectures have demonstrated increased parallelization efficiency and have addressed challenges in learning long-range dependencies more effectively than their recurrent counterparts. The scalability advantages have facilitated training on substantially larger datasets and deploying models with higher expressive power. Mathematically, the attention layer complexity scales as $O(n^2 \cdot d)$ in both time and storage, where n is the sequence length and d is the dimensionality, which surpasses the linear complexity $O(n \cdot d^2)$ in terms of layer-wise operations present in RNNs, yet the lack of recurrence allows significant parallel computations.

Python Code Snippet

Below is a Python code snippet that encompasses the core computational elements of attention mechanisms and Transformer architecture including scaled dot-product attention, multi-head attention, self-attention, feed-forward neural networks, and positional encoding.

```python
import numpy as np

def scaled_dot_product_attention(Q, K, V, d_k):
    '''
    Compute the scaled dot-product attention
    :param Q: Query matrix
    :param K: Keys matrix
    :param V: Values matrix
    :param d_k: Dimension of keys
    :return: Output of attention
    '''
    scores = np.matmul(Q, K.T) / np.sqrt(d_k)
    weights = softmax(scores)
    return np.matmul(weights, V)

def softmax(x):
    '''
    Compute softmax of vector x
    :param x: Input vector
    :return: Softmax applied vector
    '''
    e_x = np.exp(x - np.max(x))
    return e_x / e_x.sum(axis=-1, keepdims=True)

def multi_head_attention(Q, K, V, d_k, num_heads):
    '''
    Compute multi-head attention
    :param Q: Query matrix
    :param K: Keys matrix
    :param V: Values matrix
    :param d_k: Dimension of keys
    :param num_heads: Number of attention heads
    :return: Concatenated attention output
    '''
    heads = []
    for _ in range(num_heads):
        head = scaled_dot_product_attention(Q, K, V, d_k)
        heads.append(head)
    return np.concatenate(heads, axis=-1)

def feed_forward_network(x, W1, b1, W2, b2):
    '''
    Feed-forward neural network layer
```

```
    :param x: Input to the layer
    :param W1, W2: Weight matrices
    :param b1, b2: Bias vectors
    :return: Output of the feed-forward layer
    '''
    relu_output = np.maximum(0, np.dot(x, W1) + b1)
    return np.dot(relu_output, W2) + b2

def positional_encoding(position, d_model):
    '''
    Calculate positional encoding for the transformer
    :param position: Position in sequence
    :param d_model: Dimension of the model
    :return: Positional encoding vector
    '''
    pe = np.zeros((position, d_model))
    for pos in range(position):
        for i in range(0, d_model, 2):
            pe[pos, i] = np.sin(pos / (10000 ** ((2 * i) /
            ↪  d_model)))
            pe[pos, i + 1] = np.cos(pos / (10000 ** ((2 * (i + 1)) /
            ↪  d_model)))
    return pe

# Example usage with dummy data
Q = np.random.rand(5, 64) # Queries
K = np.random.rand(5, 64) # Keys
V = np.random.rand(5, 64) # Values
d_k = 64
num_heads = 8

attention_output = multi_head_attention(Q, K, V, d_k, num_heads)
print("Multi-head Attention Output", attention_output)
pos_encoding = positional_encoding(5, 64)
print("Positional Encoding", pos_encoding)
```

This code defines several key functions necessary for implementing and understanding Transformer models:

- `scaled_dot_product_attention` function computes the core attention mechanism using query, key, and value matrices.

- `softmax` is a helper function to apply the softmax operation on a vector, which is essential in computing attention weights.

- `multi_head_attention` demonstrates the parallel computation of several attention mechanisms and concatenation of their outputs.

- `feed_forward_network` simulates the position-wise feed-forward layer present in Transformer architectures.

- `positional_encoding` generates a positional encoding matrix that injects sequence information into the model.

The final block of code provides examples of computing multi-head attention and positional encoding with dummy input data.

Chapter 16

Generative Models: VAEs and GANs

Variational Autoencoders (VAEs)

Variational Autoencoders (VAEs) stand as a foundational approach in generative modeling, leveraging principles from both deep learning and variational inference. The core idea behind VAEs is to encode input data into a probabilistic latent space that can be sampled from to generate new data.

The VAE comprises an encoder-decoder architecture where the encoder maps input data x to a latent representation z, modeled as a random variable. Mathematically, this is represented as:

$$q_\phi(z \mid x) = \mathcal{N}(z; \mu_\phi(x), \Sigma_\phi(x))$$

where $\mu_\phi(x)$ and $\Sigma_\phi(x)$ are the encoder outputs, parameterized by ϕ. The decoder then reconstructs the data from z, defined by the likelihood $p_\theta(x \mid z)$.

The objective is to maximize the marginal likelihood of the data $p_\theta(x)$. As direct computation is intractable, VAEs optimize a variational lower bound known as the Evidence Lower Bound (ELBO):

$$\mathcal{L}_{\text{VAE}} = \mathbb{E}_{q_\phi(z|x)} \left[\log p_\theta(x \mid z) \right] - \text{KL} \left(q_\phi(z \mid x) \parallel p(z) \right)$$

The first term of the ELBO represents the reconstruction loss, while the second term, the Kullback-Leibler divergence, imposes a regularizing effect ensuring the posterior distribution aligns with a prior $p(z)$, often chosen to be standard normal.

Training stability in VAEs depends crucially on the choice of architectures for $\mu_\phi(x)$, $\Sigma_\phi(x)$, and $p_\theta(x \mid z)$. The `reparameterization trick`, which expresses $z = \mu_\phi(x) + \Sigma_\phi(x) \odot \epsilon$ where $\epsilon \sim \mathcal{N}(0, I)$, is essential to allow gradient-based optimization.

Generative Adversarial Networks (GANs)

Generative Adversarial Networks (GANs), introduced to mitigate the challenges in traditional generative models, employ a minimax game between two adversaries: the generator and the discriminator. The generator $G(z; \theta_g)$ maps latent variables z from a prior distribution $p_z(z)$ to the data space, while the discriminator $D(x; \theta_d)$ differentiates between real and generated data.

The GAN training objective is as follows:

$$\min_G \max_D \mathbb{E}_{x \sim p_{\text{data}}(x)}[\log D(x)] + \mathbb{E}_{z \sim p_z(z)}[\log(1 - D(G(z)))]$$

Here, $D(x)$ tries to maximize the probability of correctly classifying real versus generated data, while $G(z)$ attempts to maximize the probability of D misclassifying generated data as real.

1 Training Stability and Mode Collapse

GANs are notorious for their training instability and issues such as mode collapse, where the generator finds a small subset of the input space that fools the discriminator, yielding less diverse samples. Convergence in GANs is not guaranteed, making it crucial to implement strategies that stabilize training. Techniques including `instance normalization`, `label smoothing`, and `gradient penalty` have shown promise in counteracting instability.

One formal approach to address training instability involves the `Wasserstein GAN` (WGAN) framework, which replaces the Jensen-Shannon divergence with the Earth-Mover distance:

$$W(p_{\text{data}}, p_G) = \inf_{\gamma \in \Pi(p_{\text{data}}, p_G)} \mathbb{E}_{(x,y) \sim \gamma}[\|x - y\|]$$

where $\Pi(p_{\text{data}}, p_G)$ denotes the set of joint distributions with marginals p_{data} and p_G. This alteration leads to more stable gradients and training dynamics.

Furthermore, `Mode sharing mechanisms`, such as `unrolled GANs`, are designed to simulate the effect of the generator's future learning trajectory, thereby encouraging the generation of a broader diversity of samples, counteracting mode collapse.

Variational Autoencoders and Generative Adversarial Networks represent two principal methodologies that propel forward modern generative models. While VAEs leverage probabilistic frameworks to ensure stable training dynamics, GANs introduce adversarial settings fostering innovation in sample generation but necessitate additional considerations to safeguard against inherent training challenges.

Python Code Snippet

Below is a Python code snippet that encapsulates the implementation of key components pertaining to Variational Autoencoders (VAEs) and Generative Adversarial Networks (GANs), highlighting the computational processes, including the architecture setup, loss computation, and training procedure.

```python
import torch
import torch.nn as nn
import torch.optim as optim
from torch.autograd import Variable

# Variational Autoencoder components
class VAE(nn.Module):
    def __init__(self, input_dim, hidden_dim, latent_dim):
        super(VAE, self).__init__()
        self.encoder = nn.Sequential(
            nn.Linear(input_dim, hidden_dim),
            nn.ReLU(),
            nn.Linear(hidden_dim, latent_dim * 2)  # outputs both
            ↪    mean and log variance
        )
        self.decoder = nn.Sequential(
            nn.Linear(latent_dim, hidden_dim),
            nn.ReLU(),
            nn.Linear(hidden_dim, input_dim),
            nn.Sigmoid()
        )

    def reparameterize(self, mu, logvar):
        std = torch.exp(0.5 * logvar)
        eps = torch.randn_like(std)
        return mu + eps * std
```

```python
    def forward(self, x):
        x = self.encoder(x)
        mu, logvar = torch.chunk(x, 2, dim=1)
        z = self.reparameterize(mu, logvar)
        return self.decoder(z), mu, logvar

def loss_function_VAE(recon_x, x, mu, logvar):
    BCE = nn.functional.binary_cross_entropy(recon_x, x,
    ↪    reduction='sum')
    KLD = -0.5 * torch.sum(1 + logvar - mu.pow(2) - logvar.exp())
    return BCE + KLD

# Generative Adversarial Network components
class Generator(nn.Module):
    def __init__(self, latent_dim, output_dim):
        super(Generator, self).__init__()
        self.main = nn.Sequential(
            nn.Linear(latent_dim, 128),
            nn.ReLU(),
            nn.Linear(128, output_dim),
            nn.Tanh()
        )

    def forward(self, x):
        return self.main(x)

class Discriminator(nn.Module):
    def __init__(self, input_dim):
        super(Discriminator, self).__init__()
        self.main = nn.Sequential(
            nn.Linear(input_dim, 128),
            nn.LeakyReLU(0.2),
            nn.Linear(128, 1),
            nn.Sigmoid()
        )

    def forward(self, x):
        return self.main(x)

def train_VAE(vae, data_loader, epochs=10, lr=1e-3):
    optimizer = optim.Adam(vae.parameters(), lr=lr)
    vae.train()
    for epoch in range(epochs):
        for batch_idx, data in enumerate(data_loader):
            data = Variable(data)
            optimizer.zero_grad()
            recon_batch, mu, logvar = vae(data)
            loss = loss_function_VAE(recon_batch, data, mu, logvar)
            loss.backward()
            optimizer.step()

def train_GAN(generator, discriminator, data_loader, epochs=10,
↪    lr=1e-3):
```

```
criterion = nn.BCELoss()
optimizer_g = optim.Adam(generator.parameters(), lr=lr)
optimizer_d = optim.Adam(discriminator.parameters(), lr=lr)
for epoch in range(epochs):
    for batch_idx, data in enumerate(data_loader):
        real_data = Variable(data)
        batch_size = real_data.size(0)

        # Train discriminator on real data
        optimizer_d.zero_grad()
        real_label = Variable(torch.ones(batch_size))
        output = discriminator(real_data).squeeze()
        loss_real = criterion(output, real_label)
        loss_real.backward()

        # Train discriminator on fake data
        noise = Variable(torch.randn(batch_size, latent_dim))
        fake_data = generator(noise)
        fake_label = Variable(torch.zeros(batch_size))
        output = discriminator(fake_data.detach()).squeeze()
        loss_fake = criterion(output, fake_label)
        loss_fake.backward()
        optimizer_d.step()

        # Update generator
        optimizer_g.zero_grad()
        output = discriminator(fake_data).squeeze()
        loss_g = criterion(output, real_label)
        loss_g.backward()
        optimizer_g.step()
```

The above code defines essential classes and functions for both
Variational Autoencoders and Generative Adversarial Networks:

- VAE class handles VAE operations, including encoding, reparameterization, and decoding.

- loss_function_VAE computes the ELBO, encapsulating reconstruction and KL divergence components.

- Generator and Discriminator classes establish GAN architecture for generating and classifying data.

- train_VAE and train_GAN functions provide training loops for optimizing respective model parameters, addressing both adversarial dynamics and probabilistic encoding.

This integration enables experimentation with sophisticated generative models via concise implementations in PyTorch.

Chapter 17

Energy-Based Models and Boltzmann Machines

Energy-Based Models

Energy-Based Models (EBMs) are a foundational framework within machine learning, offering a powerful approach for representing probabilistic systems. These models define a scalar energy function $E(\mathbf{x})$ over configurations of input data $\mathbf{x}$, where lower energy corresponds to more likely states. The core idea is to learn the energy function such that it assigns lower energies to observed (and thus desirable) data points. The probability distribution over the input space is defined using the Boltzmann distribution:

$$p(\mathbf{x}) = \frac{e^{-E(\mathbf{x})}}{Z}$$

where $Z = \sum_{\mathbf{x}} e^{-E(\mathbf{x})}$ is the partition function, ensuring the distribution sums to one. Modeling Z is challenging due to computational intractability for high-dimensional $\mathbf{x}$, which underlies many learning complexities in EBMs.

Training an EBM often involves minimizing the energy of positive samples while increasing the energy of negative samples (non-data) to create a margin between likely and unlikely data.

Boltzmann Machines

Boltzmann Machines (BMs) are a class of stochastic neural networks that are quintessential EBMs. They use a set of visible units **v** and hidden units **h**, facilitating complex dependency capture between visible variables. The energy function in Boltzmann Machines is elegantly framed as:

$$E(\mathbf{v}, \mathbf{h}) = -\sum_i \sum_j v_i W_{ij} h_j - \sum_i b_i v_i - \sum_j c_j h_j$$

Here, W_{ij} denotes the symmetric interaction term between visible unit v_i and hidden unit h_j, while b_i and c_j represent biases for visible and hidden units, respectively.

This stochastic framework allows BMs to be used for learning probability distributions over the input space, albeit with significant computational demands due to the partition function Z.

1 Restricted Boltzmann Machines

Restricted Boltzmann Machines (RBMs) are a simplified variant of Boltzmann Machines that eschew connections between hidden units to ease computation while preserving representational power. In RBMs, the energy function becomes:

$$E(\mathbf{v}, \mathbf{h}) = -\sum_i \sum_j v_i W_{ij} h_j - \sum_i b_i v_i - \sum_j c_j h_j$$

RBMs facilitate efficient Gibbs sampling due to the absence of intra-layer connections, which through contrastive divergence, offer an effective means of approximating gradients and updating model parameters without explicit computation of Z.

Training involves minimizing a target function associated to the negative log-likelihood of the data, often approached through the Contrastive Divergence algorithm (**CD-k**):

$$\nabla \log p(\mathbf{v}) \approx \langle v_i h_j \rangle_{\text{data}} - \langle v_i h_j \rangle_{\text{model}}$$

Contrastive Divergence approximates "$\langle v_i h_j \rangle_{\text{model}}$" by sampling from a k-step Gibbs chain, reducing computationally intensive full likelihood maximization.

Unsupervised Learning with Boltzmann Machines

Boltzmann Machines, particularly Restricted Boltzmann Machines, play a pivotal role in unsupervised learning, securing patterns within high-dimensional input spaces owing to their strong representational capacity. They effectively capture higher-order correlations between visible variables via integration over hidden variables.

RBMs have been foundational in deep belief networks (DBNs), where multiple RBMs are stacked, underpinning unsupervised pre-training in deep learning architectures. This has led to improvements in feature learning tasks, demonstrating their place in the modern machine-learning pipeline.

EBMs and their specializations such as RBMs continue to be a rich area of theoretical research and application, accounting for diverse characteristics in complex data, providing frameworks that marry probabilistic representation with neural network-driven optimization.

Python Code Snippet

Below is a Python code snippet that encompasses the core computational elements of Energy-Based Models and Boltzmann Machines, including the calculation of energy functions, training algorithms for Restricted Boltzmann Machines and sampling techniques.

```python
import numpy as np

class BoltzmannMachine:
    def __init__(self, num_visible, num_hidden):
        '''
        Initialize Boltzmann Machine with given visible and hidden
        ↪ units.
        :param num_visible: Number of visible units.
        :param num_hidden: Number of hidden units.
        '''
        self.num_visible = num_visible
        self.num_hidden = num_hidden
        self.weights = np.random.normal(0, 0.01, (num_visible,
        ↪ num_hidden))
        self.visible_bias = np.zeros(num_visible)
        self.hidden_bias = np.zeros(num_hidden)
```

```python
def energy(self, v, h):
    '''
    Compute the energy of the current state.
    :param v: Visible units vector.
    :param h: Hidden units vector.
    :return: Energy value.
    '''
    term1 = -np.dot(v, np.dot(self.weights, h))
    term2 = -np.dot(v, self.visible_bias)
    term3 = -np.dot(h, self.hidden_bias)
    return term1 + term2 + term3

def sample_hidden(self, v):
    '''
    Sample hidden units given visible units.
    :param v: Visible units vector.
    :return: Sampled hidden units vector.
    '''
    probabilities = self.sigmoid(np.dot(v, self.weights) +
    ↪    self.hidden_bias)
    return np.random.binomial(1, probabilities)

def sample_visible(self, h):
    '''
    Sample visible units given hidden units.
    :param h: Hidden units vector.
    :return: Sampled visible units vector.
    '''
    probabilities = self.sigmoid(np.dot(h, self.weights.T) +
    ↪    self.visible_bias)
    return np.random.binomial(1, probabilities)

@staticmethod
def sigmoid(x):
    '''
    Sigmoid activation function.
    :param x: Input value or array.
    :return: Sigmoid of input.
    '''
    return 1 / (1 + np.exp(-x))

def contrastive_divergence(self, v0, k=1):
    '''
    Perform Contrastive Divergence to update weights.
    :param v0: Initial visible layer.
    :param k: Number of Gibbs sampling steps.
    :return: Update weights, visible and hidden biases.
    '''
    v = np.copy(v0)
    ph0 = self.sample_hidden(v)
    for _ in range(k):
        h = self.sample_hidden(v)
        v = self.sample_visible(h)
```

```python
        phk = self.sample_hidden(v)

        self.weights += 0.1 * (np.outer(v0, ph0) - np.outer(v, phk))
        self.visible_bias += 0.1 * (v0 - v)
        self.hidden_bias += 0.1 * (ph0 - phk)

class RestrictedBoltzmannMachine(BoltzmannMachine):
    def __init__(self, num_visible, num_hidden):
        '''
        Initialize Restricted Boltzmann Machine.
        :param num_visible: Number of visible units.
        :param num_hidden: Number of hidden units.
        '''
        super().__init__(num_visible, num_hidden)

    def train(self, data, epochs=1000, batch_size=10):
        '''
        Train the RBM using contrastive divergence.
        :param data: Training data set.
        :param epochs: Number of training epochs.
        :param batch_size: Size of mini-batches.
        '''
        for epoch in range(epochs):
            np.random.shuffle(data)
            for i in range(0, data.shape[0], batch_size):
                batch = data[i:i+batch_size]
                for sample in batch:
                    self.contrastive_divergence(sample)
            if epoch % 100 == 0:
                print(f"Epoch {epoch}: Completed")

# Example usage
num_visible = 6
num_hidden = 3
data = np.random.binomial(1, 0.5, (100, num_visible))

rbm = RestrictedBoltzmannMachine(num_visible, num_hidden)
rbm.train(data)
```

This code defines several key components for implementing Energy-Based Models and Boltzmann Machines:

- The `BoltzmannMachine` class models the energy function and sample generation between visible and hidden units.

- The `contrastive_divergence` method performs the core training update using Contrastive Divergence to refine the model weights.

- The `RestrictedBoltzmannMachine` class specializes the Boltzmann Machine, facilitating easier computation due to the lack of connections within layers.

- The `train` method is adapted for training an RBM using mini-batch gradient descent with flexible epochs.

The final block of code provides an example of how to initialize and train an RBM using synthetic binary data.

Chapter 18

Neural Tangent Kernel and Infinite Width Networks

Neural Tangent Kernel: A Theoretical Foundation

The Neural Tangent Kernel (NTK) framework provides a rigorous theoretical lens through which to understand the behavior of neural networks in the infinite width limit. As a neural network's width tends to infinity, the network's evolution under gradient descent can be accurately captured by a linearized kernel regime. This kernel, denoted as Θ, governs the dynamics of the network's output function $f(\mathbf{x}; \theta)$.

The NTK is formally defined as:

$$\Theta(\mathbf{x}, \mathbf{x}') = \nabla_\theta f(\mathbf{x}; \theta)^\top \nabla_\theta f(\mathbf{x}'; \theta)$$

where $\mathbf{x}$ and $\mathbf{x}'$ represent input data points, and $\nabla_\theta f(\mathbf{x}; \theta)$ indicates the gradient of the network function with respect to the parameters θ. This formulation reveals that as the width increases, the gradients with respect to different parameters become uncorrelated, turning the optimization process into a linear kernel learning problem.

Training Dynamics in Infinite Width

In the infinite width setting, the training dynamics of a neural network are predominantly dictated by the NTK. At initialization, the network can be described by its NTK, Θ_0, which remains nearly constant during training, enabling a precise characterization of the network's function evolution using kernel regression. The evolution of $f_t(\mathbf{x})$, the prediction at time t, is given by:

$$f_t(\mathbf{x}) = f_0(\mathbf{x}) - \eta \sum_{t'=0}^{t-1} \Theta_0(\mathbf{x}, \mathbf{x}_{t'}) \nabla_{t'} L$$

where η is the learning rate, $\mathbf{x}_{t'}$ are the training inputs, and L denotes the loss function. The constancy of Θ_0 implies linearity, meaning the learning dynamics can be viewed through a kernel learning approach.

Implications for Generalization and Optimization

The NTK framework unveils critical insights into the generalization properties of deep neural networks. The linearized view posits that networks with sufficiently large widths inherently possess strong generalization abilities due to the smoothing property of kernels, which mitigates overfitting.

Further, understanding NTK allows for the interpretation of optimization landscapes in wide networks. The convergence rate in such networks benefits from a convex-like behavior under gradient descent, driven by the underlying kernel structure:

$$\Theta_\infty(\mathbf{x}, \mathbf{x}') \approx k_{\texttt{classical}}(\mathbf{x}, \mathbf{x}')$$

where Θ_∞ is the NTK at infinite width, often resembling classical kernels such as RBF (Radial Basis Function) or polynomial kernels, contingent on the choice of activation functions and initialization.

Practical Extensions and Network Architectures

While the theoretical appeal of NTK is evident in the context of infinitely wide networks, practical neural networks are finite. Correspondingly, the NTK framework has been extended to analyze more realistic network architectures. These extensions include considerations of finite width effects through random matrix theory and empirical findings supported by NTK-based models approximating neural networks in the overparameterized regime.

Furthermore, the architectural nuances, such as choice of activation functions and network depth, significantly influence the form and properties of the NTK. For instance, ReLU activations yield a piecewise linear NTK, affecting the smoothness and expressiveness of the resulting function space:

$$\Theta_{relu}(\mathbf{x}, \mathbf{x}') = \int \sigma'(f^{l-1}(\mathbf{x}))\sigma'(f^{l-1}(\mathbf{x}')) \, df$$

where f^{l-1} denotes the pre-activation state at layer $l-1$, and σ' is the derivative of the ReLU activation.

This foundational understanding fostered by the NTK framework catalyzes deeper investigation into network scalability, functional capacity, and the development of new architectures that leverage these theoretical insights for enhanced performance in practical applications.

Python Code Snippet

Below is a Python code snippet that captures the theoretical behavior of neural networks in the context of the Neural Tangent Kernel (NTK) framework, including kernel computation, training dynamics, and generalization aspects.

```python
import numpy as np

def neural_tangent_kernel(f, x, x_prime, theta):
    '''
    Compute the Neural Tangent Kernel for input pairs.
    :param f: Network output function.
    :param x: Input data point.
    :param x_prime: Another input data point.
    :param theta: Network parameters.
```

```
    :return: NTK value for (x, x_prime).
    '''
    grad_f_x = np.gradient(f(x, theta), theta)
    grad_f_x_prime = np.gradient(f(x_prime, theta), theta)
    return np.dot(grad_f_x, grad_f_x_prime)

def kernel_regression(f_0, eta, Theta_0, x_train, t, loss_gradient):
    '''
    Compute predictions over time using NTK-based kernel regression.
    :param f_0: Initial prediction function.
    :param eta: Learning rate.
    :param Theta_0: Initial NTK.
    :param x_train: Training data points.
    :param t: Current time/epoch.
    :param loss_gradient: Gradient of the loss function.
    :return: Prediction function at time t.
    '''
    prediction = f_0
    for t_prime in range(t):
        prediction -= eta * sum(Theta_0(x_t, x) *
        ↪  loss_gradient[t_prime]
                                 for x_t in x_train)
    return prediction

def compute_ntk_matrix(f, x_train, theta):
    '''
    Compute the NTK matrix for a training dataset.
    :param f: Network output function.
    :param x_train: Training data points.
    :param theta: Network parameters.
    :return: NTK matrix.
    '''
    n = len(x_train)
    ntk_matrix = np.zeros((n, n))
    for i in range(n):
        for j in range(n):
            ntk_matrix[i, j] = neural_tangent_kernel(f, x_train[i],
            ↪  x_train[j], theta)
    return ntk_matrix

def relu_ntk_derivative(f_l_1, sigma_prime):
    '''
    Calculate the ReLU NTK component using the derivative of
    ↪  activations.
    :param f_l_1: Pre-activation outputs of layer l-1.
    :param sigma_prime: Derivative of the ReLU activation.
    :return: NTK contribution from ReLU activations.
    '''
    return np.inner(sigma_prime(f_l_1), sigma_prime(f_l_1))

def train_network_with_ntk(x_train, y_train, f, eta, theta, epochs):
    '''
    Train a neural network using its NTK representation.
```

```
    :param x_train: Training data inputs.
    :param y_train: Training data outputs.
    :param f: Network output function.
    :param eta: Learning rate.
    :param theta: Initial parameters.
    :param epochs: Number of training epochs.
    :return: Trained network parameters.
    '''
    ntk_matrix = compute_ntk_matrix(f, x_train, theta)
    for epoch in range(epochs):
        prediction = np.array([f(x, theta) for x in x_train])
        loss = prediction - y_train
        theta -= eta * np.dot(ntk_matrix, loss)
    return theta

# Example usage of the neural tangent kernel theory
def example_nn_function(x, theta):
    '''
    Example neural network function using a basic polynomial model.
    :param x: Input data.
    :param theta: Parameters.
    :return: Network output.
    '''
    return np.dot(theta, x ** 2)  # Example polynomial feature map

# Example data and parameters
x_train = np.array([[0.1], [0.2], [0.3]])
y_train = np.array([0.05, 0.22, 0.33])
theta_initial = np.random.rand(len(x_train[0]))

# Train the network using the NTK framework
trained_theta = train_network_with_ntk(
    x_train, y_train, example_nn_function, eta=0.01,
    ↪ theta=theta_initial, epochs=100)

print("Trained Parameters:", trained_theta)
```

This code defines several key functions implementing the NTK framework and its utilization in neural network training:

- **neural_tangent_kernel** computes the NTK for a pair of inputs, highlighting parameter derivatives.

- **kernel_regression** demonstrates the theoretical NTK-based prediction update.

- **compute_ntk_matrix** creates the NTK matrix for a given dataset, crucial for kernel-based learning.

- **relu_ntk_derivative** evaluates ReLU activation contributions to the NTK.

111

- `train_network_with_ntk` facilitates training a network using NTK, employing the matrix representation for dynamic updates.

- `example_nn_function` serves as an illustrative neural network model function with polynomial features.

Incorporating NTK in machine learning models allows for significant insights into training dynamics, model generalization, and adaptability to network architecture variations, offering a robust theoretical framework for deep learning exploration.

Chapter 19

Symmetries and Invariances in Neural Networks

Theoretical Foundations of Symmetry in Neural Networks

The concept of symmetry in neural networks derives from the mathematical treatment of symmetry groups in function approximation. A symmetry group G is defined as a set of transformations under which the problem's structure remains invariant. In the context of a neural network, consider an input space $\mathcal{X}$ and an associated function $f : \mathcal{X} \to \mathbb{R}$. A transformation $g \in G$ acts on the input space, and the function f is symmetric with respect to G if:

$$f(g \cdot \mathbf{x}) = f(\mathbf{x}) \quad \forall \mathbf{x} \in \mathcal{X}, \forall g \in G$$

This invariance condition empowers the network to learn representations that are robust to transformations represented by G, facilitating better data generalization and efficiency in learning.

Exploiting Permutation Invariance

Permutation invariance is particularly significant in neural networks tailored for unordered sets, such as point clouds or molecular structures. For a neural network NN, permutation invariance implies:

$$\text{NN}(\mathbf{x}_{\pi(1)}, \mathbf{x}_{\pi(2)}, \ldots, \mathbf{x}_{\pi(n)}) = \text{NN}(\mathbf{x}_1, \mathbf{x}_2, \ldots, \mathbf{x}_n)$$

for any permutation π. This can be achieved through architectures like Deep Sets, where the network function is expressed as:

$$\text{NN}(\mathbf{x}) = \rho \left(\sum_{i=1}^{n} \phi(\mathbf{x}_i) \right)$$

where ϕ and ρ are learnable functions, and the symmetric sum operation ensures permutation invariance.

Translation Invariance with Convolutional Layers

Convolutional Neural Networks (CNNs) exploit translation invariance using convolutional layers, where the same pattern can be recognized regardless of its position in the input space. A convolutional operation is mathematically delineated as:

$$(f * g)(t) = \int_{-\infty}^{\infty} f(\tau)g(t - \tau) \, d\tau$$

Discrete convolution, relevant for digital image processing, can be succinctly expressed as:

$$(f * g)[n] = \sum_{m=-\infty}^{\infty} f[m] \cdot g[n - m]$$

This operation inherently embeds the property of translation invariance in CNN architectures, rendering them effective for tasks demanding spatial hierarchical learning.

Group Equivariant Networks

Beyond mere invariance, neural networks can be equivariant to symmetries under transformation groups. A function ψ is equivariant to G if:

114

$$\psi(g \cdot \mathbf{x}) = g' \cdot \psi(\mathbf{x}) \quad \forall g \in G$$

where g' denotes the transformation's corresponding action on the output space. Group Equivariant Convolutional Networks (G-CNNs), for instance, are designed to exploit rotational or reflectional symmetries, enhancing performance on tasks involving structured data patterns. The equivariant convolution operation used in G-CNNs can be defined for a group G as:

$$[f *_G g](x) = \sum_{y \in G} f(y)g(x^{-1}y)$$

where the transformation group G dictates the dynamic kernel sharing strategy across permutations.

Symmetry and Regularization

Regularization techniques in neural networks often leverage symmetry properties for improved generalization. Lateral inhibition or weight sharing in architectures aligns with symmetric constraints, reducing redundancy and enhancing learning efficiency. For example, consider the regularization term facilitating symmetry in weights:

$$\Omega(W) = \frac{\lambda}{2} \sum_{i \neq j} (W_i - W_j)^2$$

where W_i and W_j are weights subject to symmetry, and λ is the regularization parameter. Such techniques constrain the solution space, fostering better aligned and interpretable models while mitigating the risk of overfitting.

Applications in Physical Systems and Beyond

Symmetry considerations in neural network design extend beyond theoretical elegance and are pivotal in modeling physical phenomena that inherently exhibit symmetric properties. The universality and robustness of symmetries allow networks to capture invariant structures, as embodied in scientific applications such as physics-informed neural networks (PINNs). These networks use known

115

physical laws as constraints within the learning framework, characterized by symmetric loss functions:

$$\mathcal{L}_{\text{PINN}} = \mathcal{L}_{\text{data}} + \mathcal{L}_{\text{physics}}$$

where $\mathcal{L}_{\text{physics}}$ encodes symmetric constraints representative of conservation laws or other invariant properties.

In essence, understanding and harnessing symmetries and invariances in neural networks provide a critical avenue for advancing machine learning, prompting deeper investigations into scalable architectures and principled learning algorithms.

Python Code Snippet

Below is a Python code snippet that demonstrates key computations related to symmetries and invariances in neural networks, including permutation invariance, translation invariance via convolutional operations, and implementing a basic symmetry regularization scheme.

```python
import torch
import torch.nn as nn
import torch.nn.functional as F

def deep_sets(x):
    '''
    Implements the Deep Sets architecture for permutation
    ↪ invariance.
    :param x: Input tensor for unordered set.
    :return: Permutation invariant representation.
    '''
    phi = nn.Linear(x.size(-1), 128)
    rho = nn.Linear(128, 64)

    out = F.relu(phi(x))
    summed = torch.sum(out, dim=0)   # Permutation invariant sum
    output = F.relu(rho(summed))

    return output

class SimpleCNN(nn.Module):
    '''
    A simple CNN model to illustrate translation invariance.
    '''
    def __init__(self):
        super(SimpleCNN, self).__init__()
        self.conv1 = nn.Conv2d(1, 32, kernel_size=3, stride=1,
        ↪ padding=1)
```

```python
        self.conv2 = nn.Conv2d(32, 64, kernel_size=3, stride=1,
        ↪  padding=1)
        self.fc1 = nn.Linear(64 * 8 * 8, 128)
        self.fc2 = nn.Linear(128, 10)

    def forward(self, x):
        x = F.relu(self.conv1(x))
        x = F.max_pool2d(x, 2)  # Down-sample
        x = F.relu(self.conv2(x))
        x = F.max_pool2d(x, 2)
        x = x.view(x.size(0), -1)  # Flatten
        x = F.relu(self.fc1(x))
        x = self.fc2(x)
        return x


def symmetry_regularization(W):
    '''
    Regularization term promoting symmetry in weights.
    :param W: Weight matrix.
    :return: Symmetry regularization loss.
    '''
    lambda_reg = 0.01
    n = W.size(0)
    symmetry_term = lambda_reg * torch.sum((W[:n//2] - W[n//2:]) **
    ↪  2)
    return symmetry_term

# Example usage for permutation invariance
x_example = torch.randn(10, 20)  # Example unordered set input
deep_sets_output = deep_sets(x_example)

# Example usage for translation invariance
cnn_model = SimpleCNN()
cnn_input = torch.randn(1, 1, 32, 32)  # Example image input
cnn_output = cnn_model(cnn_input)

# Example of applying symmetry regularization
W_example = torch.randn(20, 20)  # Example weight matrix to apply
↪  regularization
sym_reg_loss = symmetry_regularization(W_example)

print("Deep Sets Output:", deep_sets_output)
print("CNN Output Shape:", cnn_output.shape)
print("Symmetry Regularization Loss:", sym_reg_loss)
```

This code defines and illustrates the implementation of neural network architectures and regularization techniques based on symmetry principles:

- **deep_sets** function implements the Deep Sets architecture for creating permutation invariant representations of unordered data.

- `SimpleCNN` is a simple Convolutional Neural Network model showing how convolutional layers introduce translation invariance.

- `symmetry_regularization` function provides a regularization term designed to promote symmetry in a weight matrix, reducing redundancy.

These examples highlight crucial techniques used in designing neural networks with specific invariance properties, facilitating efficient and generalized learning.

Chapter 20

Optimization Beyond Gradient Descent

Evolutionary Algorithms and Population-Based Search

Evolutionary algorithms (EAs) form a class of optimization algorithms inspired by the theory of natural selection. These algorithms do not rely on gradient information, making them advantageous for optimizing non-differentiable, noisy, or multimodal functions. The basic structure of an EA encompasses initialization, selection, crossover, mutation, and replacement.

Given a population of solutions $\mathcal{P} = \{\mathbf{x}_1, \mathbf{x}_2, \ldots, \mathbf{x}_N\}$, each individual $\mathbf{x}_i$ is evaluated based on a fitness function $f(\mathbf{x})$. The selection process rewards superior solutions with higher probabilities of breeding. Assume that $\texttt{select}$ denotes the selection mechanism:

$$\texttt{select}(\mathcal{P}) \rightarrow \{\mathbf{y}_1, \mathbf{y}_2, \ldots, \mathbf{y}_M\}$$

Crossover operators combine pairs of selected individuals to generate offspring, defined as:

$$\texttt{crossover}(\mathbf{y}_i, \mathbf{y}_j) \rightarrow \mathbf{o}_k$$

Mutation introduces stochastic variation:

$$\texttt{mutate}(\mathbf{o}_k) \rightarrow \mathbf{o}'_k$$

Replacement strategies determine how new individuals update the population:

$$\mathcal{P} \leftarrow \texttt{replace}(\mathcal{P}, \mathcal{O})$$

where $\mathcal{O}$ denotes the offspring set.

Swarm Intelligence and Collective Behaviors

Swarm intelligence encompasses optimization techniques inspired by the collective behavior of decentralized, self-organized systems, prominently seen in natural phenomena such as bird flocking and fish schooling.

Particle Swarm Optimization (PSO) is a prototypical algorithm where a swarm of particles traverse the search space. Each particle updates its velocity and position according to:

$$\mathbf{v}_i(t+1) = \omega \mathbf{v}_i(t) + c_1 r_1 (\mathbf{p}_i - \mathbf{x}_i(t)) + c_2 r_2 (\mathbf{g} - \mathbf{x}_i(t))$$

$$\mathbf{x}_i(t+1) = \mathbf{x}_i(t) + \mathbf{v}_i(t+1)$$

Here, ω is the inertia weight, c_1 and c_2 are the cognitive and social coefficients, r_1 and r_2 are random variables in $[0, 1]$, $\mathbf{p}_i$ is the personal best position, and $\mathbf{g}$ is the global best.

Ant Colony Optimization (ACO) emulates the pheromone-based trail-laying behavior of ants for path finding. The probability $P_{ij}(t)$ of an ant at node i moving to node j is given by:

$$P_{ij}(t) = \frac{[\tau_{ij}(t)]^\alpha [\eta_{ij}]^\beta}{\sum_{k \in \mathcal{N}_i} [\tau_{ik}(t)]^\alpha [\eta_{ik}]^\beta}$$

where τ_{ij} is the pheromone level, η_{ij} is the heuristic information, and α, β are parameters controlling the influence of pheromone and heuristic paths.

Theoretical Underpinnings of Non-Gradient Methods

The efficacy of non-gradient-based methods can be explained through their ability to escape local optima and explore expansive search spaces. Evolutionary algorithms benefit from the exploration-exploitation balance controlled by selection pressure and the admixture of crossover and mutation.

In swarm intelligence, convergence guarantees rely on parameters like inertia weight in PSO, influencing the diversification-convergence trade-off. Rigorous analysis often utilizes Lyapunov stability and Markov chain models to characterize algorithm stability and convergence.

Non-gradient methods can be formalized in the context of stochastic optimization by interpreting population dynamics and particle trajectories as sampling processes over the search landscape. This perspective aligns them with Monte Carlo techniques, granting insight into their probabilistic exploration mechanisms.

Python Code Snippet

Below is a Python code snippet that encompasses the core computational elements of evolutionary algorithms and swarm intelligence, including initialization, selection, crossover, mutation, and mechanisms of Particle Swarm Optimization.

```python
import numpy as np

# Evolutionary Algorithm Components
def select(population, fitness_scores, num_selected):
    '''
    Select individuals based on fitness scores.
    :param population: Current population of solutions.
    :param fitness_scores: Corresponding fitness scores.
    :param num_selected: Number of individuals to select.
    :return: Selected individuals.
    '''
    selected_indices = np.argsort(fitness_scores)[-num_selected:]
    return population[selected_indices]

def crossover(parent1, parent2):
    '''
    Perform crossover between two parents.
    :param parent1: First parent individual.
    :param parent2: Second parent individual.
    :return: Generated offspring.
    '''
    crossover_point = np.random.randint(1, len(parent1))
    return np.concatenate([parent1[:crossover_point],
        ↪ parent2[crossover_point:]])
```

```python
def mutate(individual, mutation_rate=0.01):
    '''
    Mutate an individual's genes.
    :param individual: The individual to mutate.
    :param mutation_rate: Probability of mutation per gene.
    '''
    for i in range(len(individual)):
        if np.random.rand() < mutation_rate:
            individual[i] = np.random.rand()


def evolutionary_algorithm(pop_size, num_genes, num_generations,
    ↪ num_selected, mutation_rate):
    '''
    Execute the evolutionary algorithm.
    :param pop_size: Size of the population.
    :param num_genes: Number of genes in an individual.
    :param num_generations: Number of generations to evolve.
    :param num_selected: Number of individuals to select per
    ↪ generation.
    :param mutation_rate: Mutation rate per gene.
    :return: Final evolved population.
    '''
    population = np.random.rand(pop_size, num_genes)
    for _ in range(num_generations):
        fitness_scores = np.array([np.sum(ind) for ind in
        ↪ population])
        selected = select(population, fitness_scores, num_selected)
        offspring = []
        for i in range(0, num_selected, 2):
            parent1, parent2 = selected[i], selected[(i+1) %
            ↪ num_selected]
            child1 = crossover(parent1, parent2)
            child2 = crossover(parent2, parent1)
            mutate(child1, mutation_rate)
            mutate(child2, mutation_rate)
            offspring.append(child1)
            offspring.append(child2)
        population = np.array(offspring)
    return population


# Swarm Intelligence: Particle Swarm Optimization
class Particle:
    def __init__(self, num_dimensions):
        self.position = np.random.rand(num_dimensions)
        self.velocity = np.random.rand(num_dimensions)
        self.best_position = self.position.copy()
        self.best_value = float('inf')

    def update_velocity(self, global_best, inertia_weight,
        ↪ cognitive_coeff, social_coeff):
        r1, r2 = np.random.rand(), np.random.rand()
        cognitive_component = cognitive_coeff * r1 *
        ↪ (self.best_position - self.position)
```

```
            social_component = social_coeff * r2 * (global_best -
            ↪  self.position)
            self.velocity = inertia_weight * self.velocity +
            ↪  cognitive_component + social_component

    def update_position(self):
        self.position += self.velocity

def particle_swarm_optimization(num_particles, num_dimensions,
↪  num_iterations, inertia_weight, cognitive_coeff, social_coeff):
    '''
    Execute the particle swarm optimization algorithm.
    :param num_particles: Number of particles in the swarm.
    :param num_dimensions: Dimension of the search space.
    :param num_iterations: Number of iterations for optimization.
    :param inertia_weight: Inertia weight for velocity update.
    :param cognitive_coeff: Cognitive coefficient.
    :param social_coeff: Social coefficient.
    :return: Best position found by the swarm.
    '''
    swarm = [Particle(num_dimensions) for _ in range(num_particles)]
    global_best = min(swarm, key=lambda p:
    ↪  np.sum(p.position)).position.copy()
    for _ in range(num_iterations):
        for particle in swarm:
            fitness_value = np.sum(particle.position)
            if fitness_value < particle.best_value:
                particle.best_value = fitness_value
                particle.best_position = particle.position.copy()
            if fitness_value < np.sum(global_best):
                global_best = particle.position.copy()
            particle.update_velocity(global_best, inertia_weight,
            ↪  cognitive_coeff, social_coeff)
            particle.update_position()
    return global_best

# Run examples
final_population = evolutionary_algorithm(pop_size=50, num_genes=10,
↪  num_generations=100, num_selected=20, mutation_rate=0.01)
best_position = particle_swarm_optimization(num_particles=30,
↪  num_dimensions=10, num_iterations=100, inertia_weight=0.7,
↪  cognitive_coeff=1.5, social_coeff=1.5)

print("Final Population from Evolutionary Algorithm:\n",
↪  final_population)
print("Best Position from Particle Swarm Optimization:\n",
↪  best_position)
```

This code defines essential functions and classes for running evolutionary algorithms and Particle Swarm Optimization:

- select, crossover, and mutate functions are crucial for

managing populations in evolutionary algorithms.

- `evolutionary_algorithm` orchestrates the complete evolutionary process including selection, crossover, and mutation.

- `Particle` class holds the attributes and methods for particles in the PSO algorithm, enabling velocity and position updates.

- `particle_swarm_optimization` manages the iterative optimization process, leveraging the collective behavior of the swarm to find the global optimum.

Examples are provided to demonstrate running these algorithms, resulting in either the evolved population or the best solution found.

Chapter 21

Adversarial Examples and Model Robustness

Theoretical Foundations of Adversarial Vulnerabilities

Neural networks have shown remarkable capabilities across various tasks but remain susceptible to adversarial examples. Consider a neural network function $f : \mathbb{R}^n \to \mathbb{R}^m$, parameterized by θ, such that $f(\mathbf{x}) = \mathbf{y}$. An adversarial example is a perturbed input $\mathbf{x}' = \mathbf{x} + \delta$ where δ is crafted to cause misclassification:

$$f(\mathbf{x}') \neq f(\mathbf{x})$$

The perturbation δ is often imperceptible, constrained by some ϵ norm, leading to $\|\delta\|_p < \epsilon$. The existence of adversarial examples can be attributed to the linear nature of deep networks. The analysis can be simplified by considering the linearization of f around $\mathbf{x}$:

$$f(\mathbf{x} + \delta) \approx f(\mathbf{x}) + \nabla f(\mathbf{x}) \cdot \delta$$

The gradient $\nabla f(\mathbf{x})$ indicates sensitivity to adversarial perturbations.

Robustness Metrics and Evaluation

Robustness of a neural network to adversarial attacks can be quantified using different metrics. A common approach is to measure the worst-case perturbation δ norm within a budget ϵ that causes misclassification. A model $f(\cdot)$ is considered robust if:

$$f(\mathbf{x} + \delta) = f(\mathbf{x}) \quad \forall \|\delta\|_p < \epsilon$$

Another approach involves robustness certification, employing formal verification to show that for certain inputs, no adversarial perturbation within a given ϵ norm leads to a different classification. The robustness radius $r(\mathbf{x})$, maximal ϵ such that $f(\mathbf{x} + \delta) = f(\mathbf{x})$, is a critical measure.

Strategies to Enhance Robustness

Numerous strategies have been developed to bolster the robustness of neural networks against adversarial threats. Key approaches include:

1 Adversarial Training

Adversarial training augments the training dataset with adversarial examples to improve resilience. It formulates a min-max optimization problem:

$$\min_{\theta} \mathbb{E}_{(\mathbf{x},y) \sim \mathcal{D}} \left[\max_{\|\delta\|_p < \epsilon} \mathcal{L}(f(\mathbf{x} + \delta; \theta), y) \right]$$

where $\mathcal{L}$ denotes the loss function. This process effectively teaches the model to withstand adversarial perturbations.

2 Regularization Techniques

Regularization methods, such as adding noise during training, can also enhance robustness. For instance, noise injection can be represented by:

$$\widetilde{\mathbf{x}} = \mathbf{x} + \xi, \quad \xi \sim \mathcal{N}(0, \sigma^2 I)$$

Training on such perturbed inputs induces smoothness and reduces sensitivity to small ϵ perturbations.

3 Gradient Masking and Obfuscation

Gradient masking involves altering the decision boundaries to reduce the effectiveness of attack algorithms that rely on gradient information. This technique requires meticulous design to ensure that:

$$\nabla_{\mathbf{x}} f(\mathbf{x}) = \mathbf{0} \quad \text{where} \quad f(\mathbf{x}) = \texttt{const}$$

A network achieving gradient masking has reduced vulnerability to gradient-based attacks but may still face transferability issues.

Formal Verification and Theoretical Guarantees

The deployment of formal verification tools provides theoretical guarantees concerning the robustness of neural networks. Such methods involve constructing proofs that for specific inputs, the network remains invariant to any perturbation within a predetermined threshold. Approaches such as abstract interpretation and mixed integer linear programming (MILP) are increasingly adopted to formalize:

$$\forall \|\delta\|_p < \epsilon, \quad f(\mathbf{x} + \delta) = f(\mathbf{x})$$

Verification frameworks offer rigorous means of certifying neural network robustness and remain an active area of research.

Python Code Snippet

Below is a Python code snippet that provides a comprehensive outline of vulnerability analysis and enhancement strategies against adversarial examples in neural networks. The code covers adversarial example generation, adversarial training, and basic robustness evaluation.

```python
import torch
import torch.nn as nn
import torch.optim as optim
from torch.autograd import Variable

# Define a simple neural network for demonstration
class SimpleNN(nn.Module):
```

```python
    def __init__(self):
        super(SimpleNN, self).__init__()
        self.fc = nn.Linear(2, 2)

    def forward(self, x):
        return self.fc(x)

# Function to create adversarial example
def create_adversarial_example(model, x, y_true, epsilon, loss_fn):
    x_adv = Variable(x.data, requires_grad=True)
    y_pred = model(x_adv)
    loss = loss_fn(y_pred, y_true)
    loss.backward()
    x_adv_grad = torch.sign(x_adv.grad.data)
    x_adv = x_adv + epsilon * x_adv_grad
    return x_adv

# Function to perform adversarial training
def adversarial_training(model, data, targets, epsilon, loss_fn,
↪  optimizer):
    model.train()
    for x, y in zip(data, targets):
        x_adv = create_adversarial_example(model, x, y, epsilon,
        ↪  loss_fn)
        optimizer.zero_grad()
        y_pred_adv = model(x_adv)
        loss = loss_fn(y_pred_adv, y)
        loss.backward()
        optimizer.step()

# Simple evaluation function to measure robustness
def evaluate_robustness(model, data, targets, epsilon, loss_fn):
    model.eval()
    correct = 0
    for x, y in zip(data, targets):
        x_adv = create_adversarial_example(model, x, y, epsilon,
        ↪  loss_fn)
        y_pred_adv = model(x_adv)
        _, predicted = torch.max(y_pred_adv.data, 1)
        if predicted == y:
            correct += 1
    accuracy = 100 * correct / len(data)
    return accuracy

# Initialize model, loss function, and optimizer
model = SimpleNN()
loss_fn = nn.CrossEntropyLoss()
optimizer = optim.SGD(model.parameters(), lr=0.01)

# Dummy dataset for demonstration
data = [torch.tensor([[0.5, 0.5]], dtype=torch.float32),
        torch.tensor([[1.0, 1.0]], dtype=torch.float32)]
targets = [torch.tensor([1]), torch.tensor([0])]
```

```
# Adversarial training
adversarial_training(model, data, targets, epsilon=0.1,
↪   loss_fn=loss_fn, optimizer=optimizer)

# Evaluate robustness
accuracy = evaluate_robustness(model, data, targets, epsilon=0.1,
↪   loss_fn=loss_fn)
print("Adversarial Robustness Accuracy:", accuracy)
```

This code defines critical components necessary to understand and mitigate adversarial vulnerabilities in neural networks:

- **SimpleNN** demonstrates a basic neural network architecture for adversarial analysis.

- **create_adversarial_example** generates adversarial examples using gradient sign methods.

- **adversarial_training** augments the training process with adversarial examples to improve model resilience.

- **evaluate_robustness** measures the model's robustness by evaluating performance against adversarial examples.

The provided functions enable an understanding of how adversarial vulnerabilities manifest and can be reduced through adversarial training and evaluation.

Chapter 22

Continual Learning and Catastrophic Forgetting

Foundations of Continual Learning

Traditional machine learning paradigms typically assume that training data is static and fully available. In contrast, continual learning (CL) examines a scenario where data arrives sequentially, and models are updated incrementally. Formally, consider a sequence $\{\mathcal{D}_t\}_{t=1}^T$ of datasets presented to a neural network model f_θ parameterized by θ. Each dataset $\mathcal{D}_t$ corresponds to a unique task that the model must learn over time.

The principal challenge in CL is catastrophic forgetting, where learning new tasks $\mathcal{D}_t$ deteriorates performance on previously learned tasks $\mathcal{D}_1, \ldots, \mathcal{D}_{t-1}$. Mathematically, catastrophic forgetting can be conceptualized as an increase in loss:

$$\forall i < t, \quad \mathcal{L}_i(f_{\theta_t}) > \mathcal{L}_i(f_{\theta_i})$$

where θ_t denotes the model parameters after learning task t.

Theoretical Analysis of Catastrophic Forgetting

Catastrophic forgetting arises primarily due to overlapping representations in neural network parameters while sequentially learning multiple tasks. This overlap can be understood as interference in the parameter space. For any two tasks t_1 and t_2, catastrophic forgetting occurs when optimization for task $\mathcal{D}_{t_2}$ negatively impacts solutions beneficial for task $\mathcal{D}_{t_1}$.

Assume tasks reside in overlapping linear subspaces of parameter space. For a parameter update $\Delta\theta$ derived using gradient descent to minimize loss for task $\mathcal{D}_{t_2}$:

$$\Delta\theta = -\eta\nabla_\theta\mathcal{L}_{t_2}(f_\theta)$$

where η is the learning rate. If $\Delta\theta$ projects onto a critical direction for $\mathcal{D}_{t_1}$, forgetting occurs as gradients from $\mathcal{L}_{t_2}$ conflict with past task optimizations.

Mitigation Strategies

Various strategies have been developed to mitigate catastrophic forgetting. These strategies broadly fall into regularization-based, architecture-based, and replay-based approaches:

1   Regularization-Based Approaches

Regularization methods involve constraining updates to prevent detrimental changes in the model weights important for previous tasks. For example, Elastic Weight Consolidation (EWC) introduces a regularizer $\Omega(\theta)$ into the loss function such that:

$$\mathcal{L}_{EWC}(\theta) = \mathcal{L}_t(\theta) + \sum_{i=1}^{|\theta|} \frac{\lambda}{2}F_i(\theta_i - \theta_i^*)^2$$

where F_i is the Fisher information matrix, capturing the sensitivity of the learned weights θ_i^* from prior tasks, and λ is a hyperparameter controlling the penalty strength.

2   Architecture-Based Approaches

Architecture-based strategies involve dynamically adapting the model's architecture to accommodate new tasks without interference. For instance, Progressive Neural Networks allocate new neural columns for each incoming task $\mathcal{D}_t$, with lateral connections to previous columns:

$$f_\theta^t(x) = \sum_{i=1}^{t} g_i \circ f_{\theta_i}(x)$$

Each function f_{θ_i} corresponds to a column, while g_i parametrize lateral connections, thereby allowing task-specific subnetworks.

3   Replay-Based Approaches

Replay-based methods interleave new task data with stored samples from past tasks, preventing forgetting by periodically retraining on historical data. Memory replay can be implemented with:

$$\mathcal{L}_{replay}(\theta) = \mathcal{L}_t(\theta) + \lambda \sum_{i=1}^{k} \mathcal{L}_i(\theta|\mathcal{M}_i)$$

where $\mathcal{M}_i$ is a replay buffer for task i with balancing coefficient λ.

Optimization Challenges and Future Directions

Optimization in a continual learning context entails balancing stability and plasticity. That is, retaining prior knowledge while being adaptable to new tasks. This balance poses a continuous challenge given the evolving task distributions and computational constraints. Effective optimization strategies need to ensure efficiency without exorbitant memory footprint or excess computational cost.

Solutions incorporating meta-learning frameworks are promising, beginning to tackle transfer and shared feature extraction across tasks, thereby ideally learning task-agnostic updates that retain critical information and minimize interference in parameter space.

Python Code Snippet

Below is a Python code snippet that implements essential algorithms and theoretical calculations regarding continual learning and catastrophic forgetting, including task optimization, regularization strategies, and dynamic memory replay.

```python
import numpy as np

class ContinualLearningModel:
    def __init__(self, input_size, num_tasks):
        '''
        Initialize a continual learning model with given input size
        ↪ and number of tasks.
        :param input_size: The size of the input data.
        :param num_tasks: The number of tasks to be learned
        ↪ sequentially.
        '''
        self.input_size = input_size
        self.num_tasks = num_tasks
        # Initialize weights and biases for simplicity
        self.weights = np.random.rand(input_size)
        self.biases = np.random.rand()

    def update_parameters(self, gradient, learning_rate):
        '''
        Update model parameters using gradient descent.
        :param gradient: A list of gradients for current task.
        :param learning_rate: The learning rate.
        '''
        self.weights -= learning_rate * gradient
        self.biases -= learning_rate * np.sum(gradient)

    def apply_ewc_regularization(self, prior_params, importances,
    ↪ lambda_coefficient):
        '''
        Apply Elastic Weight Consolidation regularization.
        :param prior_params: Dictionary of parameters from prior
        ↪ tasks.
        :param importances: Dictionary of importance values for each
        ↪ parameter.
        :param lambda_coefficient: The regularization strength.
        '''
        regularization_loss = 0
        for i, weight_value in enumerate(self.weights):
            regularization_loss += lambda_coefficient *
                ↪ importances['weights'][i] * (weight_value -
                ↪ prior_params['weights'][i])**2

        self.weights -= lambda_coefficient * regularization_loss
```

```python
def dynamic_memory_replay(self, historical_data, replay_rate):
    '''
    Implement a dynamic memory replay strategy.
    :param historical_data: Stored samples from past tasks.
    :param replay_rate: The fraction of historical data used in
    ↪   the training update.
    '''
    sample_size = int(len(historical_data) * replay_rate)
    replay_samples = historical_data[:sample_size]
    # Simplified retraining routine
    self.weights = self.weights * 0.9 + np.mean(replay_samples,
    ↪   axis=0) * 0.1

# Example: training a model on several sequential tasks
def train_continual_learning_model():
    ''' A simulated training routine for a continual learning setup.
    ↪   '''
    model = ContinualLearningModel(input_size=10, num_tasks=5)
    prior_params = {'weights': model.weights.copy()}
    importances = {'weights': np.random.rand(10)}

    tasks_data = [np.random.rand(10) for _ in range(50)]  # Dummy
    ↪   tasks data
    historical_data = []

    for task in range(model.num_tasks):
        for data in tasks_data:
            # Simulated gradient computation
            gradient = np.random.rand(10)
            model.update_parameters(gradient, learning_rate=0.01)

        # Apply EWC regularization after each task
        model.apply_ewc_regularization(prior_params, importances,
        ↪   lambda_coefficient=0.1)

        # Store task data and perform memory replay
        historical_data.extend(tasks_data)
        model.dynamic_memory_replay(historical_data,
        ↪   replay_rate=0.1)

train_continual_learning_model()
```

This code defines several fundamental components crucial for understanding and implementing continual learning strategies:

- **ContinualLearningModel** class encapsulates a basic continual learning system with parameter update functionalities.

- **update_parameters** function performs parameter updates via gradient descent for the current task, aiding in accommodating new learnings.

- `apply_ewc_regularization` incorporates the Elastic Weight Consolidation technique to regularize and retain information from prior tasks.

- `dynamic_memory_replay` simulates a strategy to replay previously seen task data dynamically, helping mitigate forgetting.

- `train_continual_learning_model` sets up a mock iterative training process over several tasks using the specified learning model.

By using this framework, it allows experiments in mitigating catastrophic forgetting, thus enhancing learning efficiency across sequential tasks.

Chapter 23

Sparse Coding and Compressed Representations

Theoretical Foundations of Sparse Coding

Sparse coding utilizes the principle of sparsity to develop efficient representations of data. By assuming that a small number of latent factors can represent the observed variables, sparse coding seeks an optimal encoding matrix $\mathbf{W}$ and a sparse coding matrix $\mathbf{H}$ such that:

$$\mathbf{X} \approx \mathbf{WH}$$

where $\mathbf{X} \in \mathbb{R}^{n \times p}$ is the input data with n samples and p features, $\mathbf{W} \in \mathbb{R}^{p \times k}$ denotes the dictionary matrix, and $\mathbf{H} \in \mathbb{R}^{k \times n}$ is the sparse code matrix. The goal is to minimize the reconstruction error subject to sparsity constraints, typically formulated as:

$$\underset{\mathbf{W},\mathbf{H}}{\arg\min} \quad ||\mathbf{X} - \mathbf{WH}||_F^2 + \lambda ||\mathbf{H}||_1$$

where $||\cdot||_F$ is the Frobenius norm, and $||\cdot||_1$ enforces sparsity on the columns of $\mathbf{H}$.

Implications of Sparsity in Neural Networks

Sparsity plays a crucial role in enhancing model efficiency and interpretability within neural networks. When incorporated into neural network architectures, sparsity constraints promote the selection of a minimal subset of neurons or connections that are most informative for the task at hand.

The use of sparse regularization, such as L1 regularization, in neural networks can be defined mathematically as:

$$\mathcal{L}_{\text{total}} = \mathcal{L}_{\text{task}} + \beta ||\mathbf{W}||_1$$

where $\mathcal{L}_{\text{task}}$ is the task-specific loss function, and β controls the strength of sparsity imposed on the weights $\mathbf{W}$.

Compressed Representations and Efficiency

The application of sparse coding principles leads to compressed representations that confer computational advantages. Sparse representations enable efficient storage, faster computation, and reduced memory usage, which are particularly beneficial for deploying models on resource-constrained devices.

In deep learning, a sparse autoencoder seeks to learn a compressed representation $\mathbf{z}$ by imposing sparsity in its hidden layers:

$$\underset{\theta}{\text{argmin}} \quad ||\mathbf{x} - \hat{\mathbf{x}}||_2^2 + \lambda \sum_i \text{KL}(\rho||\hat{\rho}_i)$$

where $\mathbf{x}$ and $\hat{\mathbf{x}}$ are the input and reconstructed outputs, respectively; θ encompasses the parameters of the autoencoder; $\text{KL}(\rho||\hat{\rho}_i)$ is the Kullback-Leibler divergence for enforcing sparsity at neuron i; ρ is the target sparsity level, and $\hat{\rho}_i$ represents the actual average activation.

Interpretability through Sparse Coding

Sparse representations also contribute to model interpretability by revealing dominant features or components. The sparsity constraint on learning problems encourages solutions that uncover the underlying structures and patterns, facilitating human interpretation.

The activation of sparse codes can be visualized or related to specific input features, aiding in understanding model decisions. Consider a sparse learned dictionary $\mathbf{W}$, wherein each basis vector corresponds to a significant component of the data. The learned sparse codes $\mathbf{H}$ suggest which bases are combined to represent each data point, allowing insight into the most influential factors in the model's decision processes.

Sparse coding frameworks inherently encourage disentanglement of underlying generative factors, furthering transparency and the capacity to interpret complex models used in practice.

Python Code Snippet

Below is a Python code snippet that encompasses the core computational elements of sparse coding, sparse neural network regularization, and compressed representations, including their applications in data compression and interpretability.

```python
import numpy as np
from scipy.optimize import minimize
from sklearn.decomposition import SparseCoder
from sklearn.neural_network import MLPRegressor

def sparse_coding(X, n_components, alpha):
    '''
    Perform sparse coding on the input data.
    :param X: Input data matrix.
    :param n_components: Number of sparse atoms.
    :param alpha: Sparsity regularization parameter.
    :return: Dictionary matrix W and sparse code matrix H.
    '''
    coder = SparseCoder(n_components=n_components,
    ↪   transform_alpha=alpha)
    H = coder.fit_transform(X)
    W = coder.components_
    return W, H

def sparse_regularization_loss(W, H, X, lambda_reg=0.1):
    '''
    Calculate loss with sparsity regularization on weights.
    :param W: Dictionary or weight matrix.
    :param H: Sparse code matrix.
    :param X: Input data matrix.
    :param lambda_reg: Regularization parameter.
    :return: Regularized loss.
```

```
            ' ' '
        reconstruction_loss = np.linalg.norm(X - np.dot(W, H), 'fro')**2
        sparsity_loss = lambda_reg * np.sum(np.abs(H))
        return reconstruction_loss + sparsity_loss


def sparse_autoencoder(X, n_hidden, sparsity_target=0.05,
↪   lambda_sparsity=1.0):
        ' ' '
        Train a sparse autoencoder to obtain compressed representations.
        :param X: Input data.
        :param n_hidden: Number of nodes in hidden layer.
        :param sparsity_target: Target sparsity level.
        :param lambda_sparsity: Sparsity regularization strength.
        :return: Encoder weights and biases.
        ' ' '
        n_samples, n_features = X.shape
        encoder = MLPRegressor(hidden_layer_sizes=(n_hidden,),
                               activation='logistic',
                               solver='adam',
                               alpha=lambda_sparsity,
                               batch_size='auto',
                               max_iter=200,
                               random_state=42)
        encoder.fit(X, X)

        return encoder.coefs_[0], encoder.intercepts_[0]


def interpret_sparse_codes(W, H):
        ' ' '
        Interpreting the learned sparse codes.
        :param W: Learned dictionary matrix.
        :param H: Sparse code matrix.
        :return: Significant components and their contributions.
        ' ' '
        significant_components = np.argwhere(H > 0)
        interpretation = {i: W[:, i] for i, _ in significant_components}
        return interpretation


# Example usage
X = np.random.rand(10, 5)
n_components = 3
alpha = 1.0

# Perform sparse coding
W, H = sparse_coding(X, n_components, alpha)

# Calculate sparse regularization loss
loss = sparse_regularization_loss(W, H, X)

# Train a sparse autoencoder
encoder_weights, encoder_biases = sparse_autoencoder(X, n_hidden=2)

# Interpret the sparse codes
```

```
interpretation = interpret_sparse_codes(W, H)

print("Dictionary (W):", W)
print("Sparse Codes (H):", H)
print("Regularization Loss:", loss)
print("Encoder Weights:", encoder_weights)
print("Significant Components Interpretation:", interpretation)
```

This code defines several key functions necessary for implementing and utilizing sparse coding in neural networks:

- `sparse_coding` performs sparse coding on the input data, returning the dictionary and sparse code matrices.

- `sparse_regularization_loss` computes the sparse regularization loss given the dictionary, sparse codes, and input data.

- `sparse_autoencoder` trains a simple sparse autoencoder and returns the encoder weights and biases for compressed representations.

- `interpret_sparse_codes` provides insights into the significance of the learned sparse codes and their associated data components.

The final block of code demonstrates how to use these functions to perform sparse coding, compute the loss, train a sparse autoencoder, and interpret the results, providing practical insights into model interpretability and efficiency.

Chapter 24

Neural Differential Equations

Introduction to Differential Equations in Machine Learning

Differential equations form a mathematical framework that describes the continuous change of a system. Within the context of machine learning, neural ordinary differential equations (ODEs) bridge the gap between discrete neural architectures and continuous dynamical systems.

The fundamental equation of an ordinary differential equation is given by:

$$\frac{dy(t)}{dt} = f(y(t), t, \theta)$$

where $y(t)$ represents the state of the system at time t, f is a function parameterized by θ, and $\frac{dy(t)}{dt}$ is the time derivative of the state.

Neural ODEs use neural networks to parameterize the function f, allowing for the approximation of complex, dynamic processes over time. These equations are integrated using specialized numerical methods to simulate the temporal evolution of the network's state.

Neural ODEs: A Continuous Generalization of ResNets

Residual networks (ResNets), a cornerstone in deep learning, employ skip connections to alleviate the vanishing gradient problem. A residual block in a ResNet can be expressed by:

$$h_{t+1} = h_t + f(h_t, \theta_t)$$

In contrast, neural ODEs interpret this discretized update as the Euler method for the continuous transformation of $h(t)$:

$$\frac{dh(t)}{dt} = f(h(t), t, \theta)$$

This reformulation from a discrete sequence to a continuous dynamical system allows for seamless transitions between architectural depths by adjusting the integration time span instead of the discrete number of layers.

Numerical Solvers for Neural ODEs

The implementation of neural ODEs leverages numerical solvers to integrate the differential equation over the desired time interval. The selection of a numerical solver affects the stability and accuracy of the solution.

1 Euler Method

The simplest numerical method for solving ODEs is the Euler method, approximated as:

$$y_{t+1} = y_t + \Delta t \cdot f(y_t, t, \theta)$$

Here, Δt is the step size determining the resolution of the simulation.

2 Runge-Kutta Methods

More sophisticated approaches, such as the Runge-Kutta methods, enhance accuracy by considering intermediate states. The fourth-order Runge-Kutta method (RK4) is expressed as:

$$k_1 = f(y_t, t, \theta),$$

$$k_2 = f(y_t + \frac{\Delta t}{2} k_1, t + \frac{\Delta t}{2}, \theta),$$

$$k_3 = f(y_t + \frac{\Delta t}{2} k_2, t + \frac{\Delta t}{2}, \theta),$$

$$k_4 = f(y_t + \Delta t \cdot k_3, t + \Delta t, \theta),$$

$$y_{t+1} = y_t + \frac{\Delta t}{6}(k_1 + 2k_2 + 2k_3 + k_4)$$

3 Adaptive Step Size Methods

Adaptive solvers such as the Dormand-Prince method dynamically adjust the step size Δt according to the local error estimate, providing a balance between computational efficiency and solution precision.

Backpropagation Through an ODE Solver

The adjoint sensitivity method facilitates end-to-end learning in neural ODEs by efficiently computing gradients with respect to the parameters θ, initial conditions, and time points. For a system modeled by:

$$z(T) = z_0 + \int_0^T f(z(t), t, \theta) \, dt$$

The adjoint state $a(t)$ is defined as:

$$\frac{da(t)}{dt} = -a(t)^T \frac{\partial f}{\partial z}$$

The gradients with respect to the parameters are computed by:

$$\frac{d\mathcal{L}}{d\theta} = \int_T^0 a(t)^T \frac{\partial f}{\partial \theta} \, dt$$

Here, $a(t)$ joins the ODE system and updates backward in time, sharing the state memory footprint with the forward pass, mitigating issues of memory overhead common in conventional backpropagation through time.

Applications in Machine Learning

Neural ODEs capture temporal dependencies with a degree of flexibility and dynamism unmatched by fixed-depth models. In image classification, time-series prediction, and generative modeling, the adaptive nature of ODEs provides powerful temporal representations.

$$\texttt{minimize}\, (\mathbb{E}_{\text{data}}\left[-\log p(x(T)|x(0))\right])$$

These applications articulate the significance of neural ODEs as a unique and unifying toolset, integrating insights from differential equations into deep learning paradigms.

Python Code Snippet

Below is a Python code snippet that encompasses the core computational elements of neural differential equations, including the implementation of neural ODEs, numerical solvers such as Euler and Runge-Kutta methods, and the adjoint sensitivity method for backpropagation.

```python
import torch
import torch.nn as nn
import torch.optim as optim
from torchdiffeq import odeint

# Define the function f for dy/dt = f(y, t, theta)

class ODEFunction(nn.Module):
    def __init__(self):
        super(ODEFunction, self).__init__()
        self.linear = nn.Linear(1, 50)
        self.relu = nn.ReLU()
        self.output_layer = nn.Linear(50, 1)

    def forward(self, t, y):
        out = self.linear(y)
        out = self.relu(out)
        out = self.output_layer(out)
        return out

# Usage of odeint to solve the ODEs

def euler_method(ode_func, y0, t_span, step_size):
    t0, t1 = t_span
```

```python
    t_values = torch.arange(t0, t1, step_size)
    y_values = [y0]

    y = y0
    for t in t_values[:-1]:
        y = y + step_size * ode_func(t, y)
        y_values.append(y)

    return torch.stack(y_values)


# More sophisticated Runge-Kutta methods provided by torchdiffeq

def runge_kutta_method(ode_func, y0, t_span):
    t = torch.tensor([t_span[0], t_span[1]])
    y = odeint(ode_func, y0, t)
    return y


# Implementing the adjoint method for backpropagation through an ODE
#   solver

def adjoint_sensitivity(ode_func, y0, t_span, lr=0.01):
    optimizer = optim.Adam(ode_func.parameters(), lr=lr)
    criterion = nn.MSELoss()

    # Hypothetical true solution or target
    target = torch.tensor([[5.0]])

    for _ in range(100):    # Training iterations
        optimizer.zero_grad()
        y_pred = odeint(ode_func, y0, torch.tensor([t_span[0],
        ↪   t_span[1]]))
        loss = criterion(y_pred[1], target)
        loss.backward()
        optimizer.step()

    return ode_func


# Initial conditions and parameters
y0 = torch.tensor([[0.0]])
t_span = [0.0, 1.0]


# Instantiate and solve using euler method

ode_func = ODEFunction()
y_euler = euler_method(ode_func, y0, t_span, step_size=0.1)
print("Euler Method Solution:", y_euler)


# Solve using an Runge-Kutta method

y_rk = runge_kutta_method(ode_func, y0, t_span)
print("Runge-Kutta Method Solution:", y_rk)


# Train using the adjoint sensitivity method
```

```
ode_func = adjoint_sensitivity(ODEFunction(), y0, t_span)
```

This code introduces key functions and methods necessary for solving and backpropagating through neural ODEs:

- The `ODEFunction` class defines the neural network used to model the function f in the ODE.

- The `euler_method` function demonstrates a basic numerical solver for ODEs using the Euler method.

- The `runge_kutta_method` function utilizes the `torchdiffeq` package for a more accurate Runge-Kutta solver.

- The `adjoint_sensitivity` function outlines the learning framework for optimizing the parameters of the neural ODE using the adjoint sensitivity method.

The provided examples illustrate the implementation of these methods, highlighting their practical applications in the context of neural differential equations.

Chapter 25

Graph Neural Networks and Relational Learning

Graph Representation in Non-Euclidean Spaces

Graphs serve as a powerful representation of relational data, where nodes V and edges E encapsulate entities and their interactions, respectively. Graphs differ from traditional Euclidean data, necessitating the extension of neural network architectures to accommodate their topological properties. A graph is mathematically defined as $G = (V, E)$, where V is the set of vertices and $E \subseteq V \times V$ denotes the set of edges. Here, the adjacency matrix $A \in \mathbb{R}^{|V| \times |V|}$ captures the connection patterns between nodes.

Message Passing Framework

The message passing framework underlies many graph neural network (GNN) architectures, facilitating node representation learning via iterative information exchange between connected nodes. For a node $v_i \in V$, its feature vector $\mathbf{h}_i^{(k)}$ at layer k is updated based on features of its neighbors:

$$h_i^{(k+1)} = \text{UPDATE}(h_i^{(k)}, \text{AGGREGATE}(\{h_j^{(k)} \mid j \in \mathcal{N}(i)\}))$$

where $\mathcal{N}(i)$ denotes the set of neighbors of node i, and the AGGREGATE function computes a summary of the neighborhood information, often as a permutation-invariant function such as mean, sum, or max pooling. The UPDATE function typically involves neural layers to transform aggregated messages.

Spectral Graph Convolutions

Spectral graph convolutions leverage the eigen-decomposition of the graph Laplacian $L = D - A$, where D is the degree matrix. Convolution operation in the spectral domain is defined using the Fourier basis of the graph, represented by the eigenvectors of L. Letting $\hat{L} = U \Lambda U^T$ express the eigendecomposition, the convolution operation is given by:

$$\mathbf{H}^{(k+1)} = \sigma(\hat{L} \mathbf{H}^{(k)} \Theta^{(k)})$$

where $\Theta^{(k)}$ are learnable parameters and σ is an activation function.

Spatial Graph Convolutions

Spatial approaches perform convolutions directly on the graph structure, applying localized parameter sharing akin to traditional convolutions. A spatial graph convolution updates node features $\mathbf{h}_i$ by aggregating and transforming features from immediate neighbors:

$$\mathbf{h}_i^{(k+1)} = \sigma \left(\sum_{j \in \mathcal{N}(i) \cup \{i\}} \frac{1}{\sqrt{d_i d_j}} \mathbf{W}^{(k)} \mathbf{h}_j^{(k)} \right)$$

where $\mathbf{W}^{(k)}$ are filter weights and d_i is the degree of node i.

Expressive Power and Inductive Biases of GNNs

The expressive power of GNNs is fundamentally linked to their ability to capture complex relational patterns. The inductive bias of

GNNs, inheriting invariance and locality from their design, is crucial for modeling graph-structured data. A GNN's capacity to distinguish among graph structures is often equated to the Weisfeiler-Lehman graph isomorphism test, which iteratively refines node labels based on neighborhood features.

The representation capacity of GNNs can be enhanced by designing tailored AGGREGATE and UPDATE functions to inject domain-specific knowledge or using techniques like attention mechanisms to weigh contributions from different parts of the graph selectively.

Applications in Relational Learning

GNNs excel in various relational learning tasks where interactions among entities are of essence. These include node classification, where GNNs are trained to predict categorical labels for nodes based on graph context, and link prediction, which aims to infer missing connections between nodes. In the realm of non-Euclidean data structures, GNNs uncover latent representations conducive for applications ranging from social network analysis to molecule property prediction.

With their ability to generalize across various graph structures, GNNs are pivotal in advancing the frontiers of machine learning on relational data, providing a robust framework for understanding and predicting complex entities through their interactions.

Python Code Snippet

Below is a Python code snippet that encompasses the core computational elements of graph neural networks, including graph representation, message passing, and aggregation functions.

```
import numpy as np
import networkx as nx

def adjacency_matrix(graph):
    '''
    Generate the adjacency matrix for a given graph.
    :param graph: NetworkX graph object.
    :return: Adjacency matrix as numpy array.
    '''
    return nx.adjacency_matrix(graph).todense()

def message_passing(graph, features, num_layers=2):
```

```python
    '''
    Implement the message passing framework.
    :param graph: NetworkX graph object.
    :param features: Numpy array of node features.
    :param num_layers: Number of iterations for message passing.
    :return: Updated node features after message passing.
    '''
    A = adjacency_matrix(graph)
    for _ in range(num_layers):
        new_features = np.matmul(A, features)  # Aggregate
        features = new_features / new_features.sum(axis=1,
        ↪ keepdims=True)  # Normalize
    return features

def laplacian_matrix(graph):
    '''
    Compute the graph Laplacian matrix.
    :param graph: NetworkX graph object.
    :return: Laplacian matrix as numpy array.
    '''
    return nx.laplacian_matrix(graph).todense()

def spectral_convolution(graph, features, theta):
    '''
    Perform spectral graph convolution.
    :param graph: NetworkX graph object.
    :param features: Numpy array of node features.
    :param theta: Convolution parameter matrix.
    :return: Transformed features.
    '''
    L = laplacian_matrix(graph)
    eigvals, eigvecs = np.linalg.eigh(L)
    return np.matmul(eigvecs, np.matmul(np.diag(np.matmul(eigvals,
    ↪ theta)), np.matmul(eigvecs.T, features)))

def spatial_convolution(graph, features, weights):
    '''
    Perform spatial graph convolution.
    :param graph: NetworkX graph object.
    :param features: Numpy array of node features.
    :param weights: Numpy array of filter weights.
    :return: Updated features after spatial convolution.
    '''
    A = adjacency_matrix(graph)
    D = np.diag(A.sum(axis=1).flatten())
    D_inv_sqrt = np.linalg.inv(np.sqrt(D))
    normalized_A = np.matmul(D_inv_sqrt, np.matmul(A, D_inv_sqrt))
    return np.matmul(normalized_A, np.matmul(features, weights))

def aggregate_information(node_features):
    '''
    Aggregate information from node features.
    :param node_features: List of node feature vectors.
```

```
    :return: Aggregated feature vector.
    '''
    return np.sum(node_features, axis=0)

# Example usage with a simple graph and random features
G = nx.erdos_renyi_graph(5, 0.5)  # Random graph
features = np.random.rand(5, 3)  # Random features for 5 nodes with
↪  3 features each
theta = np.random.rand(3)  # Dummy parameter for spectral
↪  convolution
weights = np.random.rand(3, 3)  # Dummy weights for spatial
↪  convolution

updated_features = message_passing(G, features)
spectral_features = spectral_convolution(G, features, theta)
spatial_features = spatial_convolution(G, features, weights)
aggregated_features = aggregate_information(features)

print("Original Features:\n", features)
print("Updated Features after Message Passing:\n", updated_features)
print("Features after Spectral Convolution:\n", spectral_features)
print("Features after Spatial Convolution:\n", spatial_features)
print("Aggregated Features:\n", aggregated_features)
```

This code defines several key functions necessary for implementing graph neural network operations:

- `adjacency_matrix` generates the adjacency matrix from a NetworkX graph.

- `message_passing` simulates the iterative message passing process over the graph.

- `laplacian_matrix` computes the graph's Laplacian for spectral operations.

- `spectral_convolution` applies spectral convolution using the Laplacian's eigendecomposition.

- `spatial_convolution` carries out spatial convolution via localized parameter sharing.

- `aggregate_information` summarizes node features using sum aggregation.

The final block of code demonstrates these operations using a synthetic graph and feature set.

Chapter 26

Meta-Learning and Hypothesis Space Search

Theoretical Underpinnings of Meta-Learning

Meta-learning, often described as "learning to learn," focuses on designing models that adapt quickly to new tasks using prior experience. This adaptive learning paradigm is grounded in the idea that the model can leverage previous task information, encapsulated in a meta-knowledge, to facilitate rapid learning on novel tasks. The process can be abstracted using the concept of a meta-learner, which optimizes over a distribution of tasks $p(T)$. The objective of meta-learning can be formalized as:

$$\theta^* = \arg \min_{\theta} \mathbb{E}_{T \sim p(T)} \left[\mathcal{L}_T(\theta_T) \right]$$

Here, θ are the parameters of the meta-learner, θ_T are task-specific parameters, and $\mathcal{L}_T$ represents the task loss function. The focus is on minimizing the expected loss across multiple tasks, ultimately leading to improved performance on unseen tasks.

Bias-Variance Trade-offs in Meta-Learning

The bias-variance trade-off in meta-learning is a critical consideration, affecting the generalization ability of the learner. The decomposition of the expected error is defined as:

$$\text{Error} = \underbrace{(\text{Bias})^2}_{\text{Systematic Error}} + \underbrace{\text{Variance}}_{\text{Sensitivity to Data}} + \underbrace{\text{Irreducible Error}}_{\text{Noise}}$$

In the context of meta-learning, biases arise from over-specialization to specific tasks, while variance increases due to fluctuations across different tasks. The key challenge is to efficiently balance these components by utilizing shared structures across tasks to reduce both bias and variance simultaneously.

Fast Adaptation Mechanisms

Fast adaptation in meta-learning involves swiftly tuning the model's parameters θ_T from the meta-learned initialization θ. This balance can be achieved through various mechanisms such as gradient-based adaptations, weight updates, or dynamic parameter adjustments. A popular method for fast adaptation is Model-Agnostic Meta-Learning (MAML), where the model is trained such that a small number of gradient steps suffices for adaptation:

$$\theta_T = \theta - \alpha \nabla_\theta \mathcal{L}_T(\theta)$$

where α is the step size, learning of which optimizes the adaptation process. Through MAML, the model's initialization is configured to enable swift and efficient adaptation across diverse tasks.

Exploring Hypothesis Space

The hypothesis space $\mathcal{H}$ in meta-learning is broadened by examining the shared information among tasks. By effectively exploring this hypothesis space, the meta-learner seeks to identify a prior that encapsulates common structures. The meta-objective guides the search within this space for broadly applicable and transferable models. The fast adaptation mechanisms further narrow down from this initial prior θ to a task-specific hypothesis:

$$h_T \in \mathcal{H} \Rightarrow \mathcal{H}_T = \{\theta_T : \theta_T = f(\theta, D_T)\}$$

where f indicates a function that tailors θ to task-specific data D_T.

Scalability and Efficiency

A major challenge in meta-learning is maintaining scalability and computational efficiency, crucial for practical implementations. Advanced methods optimize the learning process through meta-optimizers, architecture searches, and efficiently utilizing task similarities. Meta-learned optimizers adapt the update rules themselves to ensure rapid convergence over task distributions.

$$\theta \leftarrow \theta - \eta \hat{\nabla}_\theta \sum_T \mathcal{L}_T(\theta_T)$$

where η is the learning rate adjusted based on the learned updates $\hat{\nabla}_\theta$. These frameworks are designed to minimize computational overhead while maximizing the efficiency of parameter updates for rapid learning.

Model Complexity and Overfitting

Managing model complexity is paramount to curtail overfitting within the meta-learning framework. Regularization techniques like dropout, L2 regularization, and early stopping are instrumental. Furthermore, controlling network complexity prevents overfitting to the meta-training set, ensuring robust generalization to novel tasks. The model's complexity is guided by:

$$\mathcal{C}(\theta) \approx ||\theta||^2 + \lambda \cdot \text{Reg}(\theta)$$

where λ is a hyperparameter balancing regularization strength. This balance ensures that learned models remain both adaptable and generalized without succumbing to the drawback of excessive parameterization.

Python Code Snippet

Below is a Python code snippet that encompasses the core computational elements related to meta-learning, detailing the optimization processes for meta-learner initialization, adaptation mechanisms, and hyperparameter tuning relevant for efficient, scalable, and robust learning across tasks.

```python
import numpy as np

def meta_loss(theta, task_distribution):
    '''
    Calculate the meta-loss across a distribution of tasks.
    :param theta: Meta-learner parameters.
    :param task_distribution: List of tasks, each with its
    ↪    corresponding data.
    :return: Meta-loss.
    '''
    total_loss = 0
    for task in task_distribution:
        theta_T = fast_adapt(theta, task)
        total_loss += task_loss(theta_T, task)
    return total_loss / len(task_distribution)

def task_loss(theta_T, task_data):
    '''
    Compute the loss for a specific task.
    :param theta_T: Parameters adapted to specific task.
    :param task_data: Data for the specific task.
    :return: Loss value.
    '''
    # Assuming a simple mean-squared error loss for demonstration
    predictions = np.dot(task_data['X'], theta_T)
    loss = np.mean((predictions - task_data['y']) ** 2)
    return loss

def fast_adapt(theta, task):
    '''
    Quickly adapt meta-learned parameters to a new task.
    :param theta: Initial parameters from the meta-learner.
    :param task: Specific task data for adaptation.
    :return: Adapted task-specific parameters.
    '''
    alpha = 0.01  # Step size
    gradients = compute_gradient(theta, task)
    theta_T = theta - alpha * gradients
    return theta_T

def compute_gradient(theta, task):
    '''
    Compute the gradient of the loss with respect to theta.
```

```python
    :param theta: Meta-learner parameters.
    :param task: Specific task data for gradient computation.
    :return: Gradient vector.
    '''
    # Placeholder for gradient computation
    # In practice, this involves backpropagation or other
    ↪    differentiation techniques
    return np.random.randn(*theta.shape)  # Random gradient for
    ↪    demonstration

def train_meta_learner(task_distribution, meta_iterations=1000):
    '''
    Train the meta-learner across a distribution of tasks.
    :param task_distribution: Distribution of tasks for
    ↪    meta-training.
    :param meta_iterations: Number of iterations for training.
    :return: Learned meta-learner parameters.
    '''
    theta = np.random.randn(10)  # Random initialization for
    ↪    demonstration
    for iteration in range(meta_iterations):
        loss = meta_loss(theta, task_distribution)
        theta -= 0.001 * compute_gradient(theta, task_distribution)
        if iteration % 100 == 0:
            print(f"Iteration {iteration}: Meta-loss = {loss}")
    return theta

# Example task distribution
tasks = [
    {'X': np.random.randn(100, 10), 'y': np.random.randn(100)} for _
    ↪    in range(5)
]

# Train the meta learner
meta_parameters = train_meta_learner(tasks)
```

This code encapsulates various essential functions and processes required to implement meta-learning and its core elements:

- **meta_loss** function computes the mean loss over a distribution of tasks used for evaluating the performance of the meta-learner.

- **task_loss** calculates the loss function for a specific task, assuming a mean-squared error loss for simplicity.

- **fast_adapt** implements the adaptation process of the meta-learner's parameters to task-specific requirements, employing gradient-based optimization.

- `compute_gradient` serves as a placeholder for gradient computation, demonstrating how gradients could be calculated for parameter updates.

- `train_meta_learner` conducts the entire training process over multiple tasks, updating the meta-learner's parameters iteratively to minimize meta-loss function.

In conclusion, each function contributes to exploring and leveraging the hypothesis space, ensuring the model rapidly adapts to new tasks, thus optimizing meta-learning effectively.

Chapter 27

Quantum Neural Networks and Computing

Foundations of Quantum Computing

Quantum computing offers a novel computational paradigm based on the principles of quantum mechanics, characterized by phenomena such as superposition and entanglement. A quantum computer operates on quantum bits or *qubits*, which unlike classical bits can represent both 0 and 1 simultaneously, thanks to their quantum states. The quantum state of a qubit can be mathematically expressed as:

$$|\psi\rangle = \alpha|0\rangle + \beta|1\rangle$$

where $|\alpha|^2 + |\beta|^2 = 1$, with α and β being complex numbers that denote the probability amplitudes.

Entanglement, a core feature of quantum mechanics, allows qubits to exhibit correlations that are stronger than any classical correlation, enabling exponentially richer state spaces than traditional binary systems. Quantum operations, typically represented as unitary matrices U, evolve quantum states via:

$$|\psi'\rangle = U|\psi\rangle$$

With quantum gates acting as reversible and linear operators, the potential to represent complex phenomena grows exponentially with the number of involved qubits.

Quantum Neural Networks (QNNs)

Quantum Neural Networks are seen as a symbiotic blend of classical neural networks and quantum mechanics, aiming to exploit quantum computing to enhance neural network capabilities. QNNs leverage quantum nodes that exploit quantum state representations and unitary transformations as activation functions or operators within the network.

The architecture of a QNN aims to encode classical information x into quantum states. This quantum encoding involves a mapping of classical data to a higher-dimensional quantum space, often executed via a quantum feature map such as:

$$|\phi(x)\rangle = U(x)|0\rangle^{\otimes n}$$

where $U(x)$ is a unitary operator encoding classical data x into the state space of n qubits.

Quantum Gates and Circuits for QNNs

Quantum gates, fundamental to the operation of QNNs, transform qubit states and form the building blocks of quantum circuits. Commonly utilized gates include Pauli gates (X, Y, Z), Hadamard gate (H), and controlled gates like CNOT. Quantum circuits, orchestrated as sequence of these gates, implement the neural-like transformations.

In the context of QNNs, each layer of the network can be seen as quantum circuits executing unitary transformations:

$$|\psi'\rangle = U_n \ldots U_2 U_1 |\psi\rangle$$

where U_i denotes the unitary operation corresponding to the i-th layer.

QNN Training Regimes

Training QNNs seeks to adjust quantum circuit parameters to minimize a given loss function. This optimization process might involve hybrid approaches combining classical optimization routines with quantum resources, given that direct parameter updates in quantum layers can be highly non-trivial due to quantum measurement constraints.

A hybrid quantum-classical approach could involve adjusting parameters θ of a quantum circuit such that:

$$\theta^* = \arg \min_{\theta} \langle \psi_{\text{out}} | L | \psi_{\text{out}} \rangle$$

where $|\psi_{\text{out}}\rangle$ is the output state of a quantum network, and L is a Hermitian operator representing the loss function.

Potential of Quantum Neural Networks

The potential of QNNs lies primarily in their ability to naturally exploit the expanded computational space provided by quantum mechanics, thereby potentially surpassing classical networks in some domains. This advantage manifests in enhanced model expressivity and the capacity to solve complex problems more efficiently, such as quantum chemistry simulations or problems involving massive linear algebra computations, which are infeasible for classical resources due to exponential state spaces.

The theoretical study of QNNs aims to uncover the precise conditions and problem domains in which quantum enhancement leads to significant advantages in both representation fidelity and computational efficiency over traditional networks. Such understanding remains an active area of research, promising transformative capabilities in artificial intelligence with growing quantum hardware maturity.

Python Code Snippet

Below is a Python code snippet that encompasses the core computational elements related to the quantum neural network architecture, including quantum state preparation, unitary transformations in quantum circuits, and the hybrid quantum-classical optimization approach for training.

```python
import numpy as np
from qiskit import QuantumCircuit, Aer, execute
from qiskit.circuit import Parameter

def initialize_qubit_state():
    '''
    Initialize a single qubit in a superposition state.
    :return: QuantumCircuit object with initialized state.
    '''
    qc = QuantumCircuit(1)
    qc.h(0)  # Apply Hadamard gate to create superposition
    return qc

def apply_entanglement(qc):
    '''
    Apply entanglement to the first two qubits of the circuit.
    :param qc: QuantumCircuit object before entanglement.
    '''
    qc.cx(0, 1)   # Apply CNOT gate for entanglement

def quantum_feature_map(x):
    '''
    Encode classical data into a quantum state.
    :param x: Classical input data.
    :return: QuantumCircuit object with data encoded.
    '''
    n = len(x)
    qc = QuantumCircuit(n)
    for i in range(n):
        qc.rx(x[i], i)   # Rotate around x-axis
    return qc

def create_qnn_layer(qc, params):
    '''
    Implement a layer of the QNN with parameterized quantum gates.
    :param qc: QuantumCircuit to apply the layer to.
    :param params: Parameters for quantum gates in the layer.
    '''
    n = qc.num_qubits
    for i in range(n):
        qc.ry(params[i], i)    # Parameterized Y rotation
        qc.cz(i, (i+1) % n)   # Controlled-Z entanglement

def measure_circuit(qc):
    '''
    Measures the qubit states of the given quantum circuit.
    :param qc: QuantumCircuit object to be measured.
    '''
    qc.measure_all()

def run_circuit(qc):
    '''
```

```
    Executes a quantum circuit on a simulator and returns the
    ↪   counts.
    :param qc: QuantumCircuit object to run.
    :return: Bitstring counts from the execution.
    '''
    simulator = Aer.get_backend('qasm_simulator')
    job = execute(qc, simulator, shots=1024)
    return job.result().get_counts()

def hybrid_classical_optimization(data, qc, params):
    '''
    Simulated minimization of a loss function involving a quantum
    ↪   circuit.
    :param data: Classical data to encode.
    :param qc: QuantumCircuit object corresponding to the QNN.
    :param params: Parameters for gate operations in the circuit.
    :return: Optimized parameter values.
    '''
    learning_rate = 0.01
    for epoch in range(100):  # Example fixed number of iterations
        feature_map = quantum_feature_map(data)
        qc = qc + feature_map
        create_qnn_layer(qc, params)
        measure_circuit(qc)
        counts = run_circuit(qc)

        # Example of a simple loss function: maximize '00'
        ↪   measurement outcome
        loss = -counts.get('00', 0)

        # Update parameters
        params = [p - learning_rate * loss for p in params]
    return params

# Running example
x_data = [0.5, -0.5, 1.0]  # Example classical data
qc = QuantumCircuit(len(x_data))
initial_params = np.random.rand(len(x_data))  # Random
↪   initialization of parameters
optimized_params = hybrid_classical_optimization(x_data, qc,
↪   initial_params)

print("Optimized Parameters:", optimized_params)
```

This code provides a comprehensive implementation of functions necessary for the setup and execution of a quantum neural network model:

- `initialize_qubit_state` creates a superposition of quantum states using the Hadamard gate.

162

- `apply_entanglement` utilizes a CNOT gate to entangle qubits, which is crucial for exploiting quantum correlations.

- `quantum_feature_map` encodes classical input data into a quantum circuit through rotations.

- `create_qnn_layer` applies parameterized quantum gates to create neural-like transformations.

- `measure_circuit` and `run_circuit` perform and simulate quantum measurements, obtaining outcome statistics.

- `hybrid_classical_optimization` implements a hybrid optimization routine, integrating classical optimization with quantum circuits to fine-tune model parameters.

The final portion of the code demonstrates a simple use case with example data and a basic optimization loop.

Chapter 28

Neuromorphic Computing and Spiking Neural Networks

Introduction to Neuromorphic Computing

Neuromorphic computing endeavors to emulate the neural architectures of biological systems in silicon-based substrates, thereby enabling machines to process information in a manner akin to biological brains. Central to this paradigm are *spiking neural networks* (SNNs), which represent a shift from the dominant rate-based models in artificial neural networks (ANNs) towards event-driven, time-dependent computations. The primary motivation is the significant energy efficiency and robust information-processing capabilities observed in biological systems.

Mathematical Modeling of Spiking Neurons

At the heart of SNNs is the spiking neuron model, which characterizes neurons using dynamic computational models that simulate the temporal aspects of biological neuronal activity. One such widely adopted model is the *Leaky Integrate-and-Fire* (LIF) neuron, mathematically represented by the differential equation:

$$\tau_m \frac{dV(t)}{dt} = -(V(t) - V_{\text{rest}}) + R_m I(t)$$

Here, $V(t)$ denotes the membrane potential at time t, τ_m is the membrane time constant, V_{rest} is the resting potential, R_m is the membrane resistance, and $I(t)$ is the input current. A spike is emitted when $V(t)$ exceeds a certain threshold V_{th}, after which $V(t)$ is reset to V_{reset}.

Network Dynamics and Synaptic Integration

The synaptic input at each neuron synapse, represented by $I(t)$, plays a crucial role in network dynamics, where synapses are often modeled via conductance-based or current-based formulations. The postsynaptic current or conductance can be expressed using exponential decay functions, defined as:

$$I_{\text{syn}}(t) = \sum_j w_j e^{-\frac{(t - t_j^f)}{\tau_{\text{syn}}}}$$

where w_j is the synaptic weight, t_j^f is the firing time of the presynaptic neuron j, and τ_{syn} is the synaptic time constant. SNNs leverage such temporal dynamics for temporal coding, where information is encoded in the precise spike timing.

Learning in Spiking Neural Networks

Learning in SNNs involves the optimization of synaptic weights to achieve specific tasks, capitalizing on algorithms inspired by *Spike-Timing-Dependent Plasticity* (STDP). An STDP rule modifies synaptic weights according to the relative timing of pre- and post-synaptic spikes, typically formulated:

$$\Delta w = A_+ e^{-\frac{\Delta t}{\tau_+}} \text{ if } \Delta t > 0 \quad \text{or} \quad \Delta w = -A_- e^{\frac{\Delta t}{\tau_-}} \text{ if } \Delta t < 0$$

where $\Delta t = t_{\text{post}} - t_{\text{pre}}$, with t_{post} and t_{pre} being the post- and pre-synaptic spike times, respectively. A_+ and A_- are scaling factors, and τ_+ and τ_- are the STDP time constants.

Implications for Biologically Inspired Computation

Spiking neural networks hold the promise of unlocking new frontiers in biologically inspired computation, attributed to their energy efficiency, temporal precision, and capacity to process spatiotemporal patterns. SNNs offer theoretical advantages in flexibly modeling real-time, asynchronous data processing scenarios akin to biological nervous systems. Neuromorphic hardware that efficiently implements SNNs provides pathways towards scalable, low-energy computing infrastructures capable of integrative processing requirements seen in sensory, motor, and cognitive tasks.

The research trajectory for SNN deployment involves further development in learning rules, network architectures, and practical implementations that maximize SNN advantages in varied computational tasks, particularly those that have classical systems outpaced due to their intrinsic parallel and temporal dynamics.

Python Code Snippet

Below is a Python code snippet that encompasses the core computational elements of spiking neural networks, including modeling of spiking neurons, network dynamics, synaptic integration, and learning rules.

```python
import numpy as np

class LeakyIntegrateAndFireNeuron:
    """
    A class representing a Leaky Integrate-and-Fire (LIF) neuron.
    """
    def __init__(self, tau_m, V_rest, V_th, V_reset, R_m):
        self.tau_m = tau_m
        self.V_rest = V_rest
        self.V_th = V_th
        self.V_reset = V_reset
        self.R_m = R_m
        self.V = V_rest

    def step(self, I, dt):
        """
        Update the neuron state for a given input current and
        ↪   timestep.
        :param I: Input current.
```

```python
        :param dt: Timestep.
        :return: True if a spike occurs, otherwise False.
        """
        dV = dt * (- (self.V - self.V_rest) + self.R_m * I) /
        ↪    self.tau_m
        self.V += dV
        spike = False
        if self.V >= self.V_th:
            self.V = self.V_reset
            spike = True
        return spike


def synaptic_input(w, t_f, tau_syn, t):
    """
    Calculate synaptic input given synaptic weight and firing time.
    :param w: Synaptic weight.
    :param t_f: Firing time of the pre-synaptic neuron.
    :param tau_syn: Synaptic time constant.
    :param t: Current time.
    :return: Synaptic input value.
    """
    return np.sum(w * np.exp(-(t - t_f) / tau_syn))


def stdp_update(w, t_post, t_pre, A_plus, A_minus, tau_plus,
↪ tau_minus):
    """
    Update the synaptic weight using STDP rule.
    :param w: Current synaptic weight.
    :param t_post: Post-synaptic spike time.
    :param t_pre: Pre-synaptic spike time.
    :param A_plus: STDP potentiation factor.
    :param A_minus: STDP depression factor.
    :param tau_plus: STDP potentiation time constant.
    :param tau_minus: STDP depression time constant.
    :return: Updated synaptic weight.
    """
    dt = t_post - t_pre
    if dt > 0:
        w += A_plus * np.exp(-dt / tau_plus)
    else:
        w -= A_minus * np.exp(dt / tau_minus)
    return w


# Example usage of LIF neuron and STDP mechanism
lif_neuron = LeakyIntegrateAndFireNeuron(
    tau_m=20.0, V_rest=-65.0, V_th=-50.0, V_reset=-65.0, R_m=10.0
)

# Simulate a neuron receiving a constant input current
input_current = 1.5
for time_step in range(100):
    spike_occurred = lif_neuron.step(input_current, dt=1.0)
    if spike_occurred:
```

```
                print(f"Spike at timestep {time_step}")

# Synaptic input calculation example
w = np.array([0.5, 0.3])
t_f = np.array([1, 2])
tau_syn = 5.0
syn_input = synaptic_input(w, t_f, tau_syn, t=10)
print("Synaptic input:", syn_input)

# STDP update example
w_initial = 0.5
t_post = 2.0
t_pre = 1.5
A_plus = 0.005
A_minus = 0.005
tau_plus = 20.0
tau_minus = 20.0
w_updated = stdp_update(w_initial, t_post, t_pre, A_plus, A_minus,
↪   tau_plus, tau_minus)
print("Updated synaptic weight:", w_updated)
```

This code defines several key components necessary for implementing spiking neural networks:

- `LeakyIntegrateAndFireNeuron` class implements a model for LIF neurons, simulating membrane potential and spike generation.

- `synaptic_input` function calculates the synaptic input current based on synaptic weights and firing times using exponential decay.

- `stdp_update` function adjusts the synaptic weights according to the spike-timing-dependent plasticity (STDP) rules.

The final block of code demonstrates a simple simulation with a neuron processing a constant input current, calculation of synaptic input value at a given time, and application of the STDP learning rule to update synaptic weights.

Chapter 29

Explainability and Interpretability in Deep Learning

Saliency Methods

The saliency of neural network outputs regarding input features provides insights into the model's decision mechanisms. Within the framework of differentiable models, saliency maps can be derived via the computation of the gradient of output with respect to input, specifically

$$S(x) = \nabla_x f(x),$$

where $f(x)$ is the model's predicted output for input x, and ∇_x denotes the gradient with respect to the input x. This approach provides pixel-wise importance scores in visual tasks, aiding in understanding which input features are pivotal for decision making. Among the techniques, `Saliency Maps`, `Guided Backpropagation`, and `Integrated Gradients` are noteworthy for their theoretical underpinnings and practical utility.

Integrated Gradients is formulated as:

$$\mathrm{IG}_i(x) = (x_i - x_i') \times \int_{\alpha=0}^{1} \frac{\partial f(x' + \alpha \times (x - x'))}{\partial x_i} d\alpha,$$

where x' is a baseline input, often chosen as a zero vector, and α is a scaling parameter.

Interpretability Metrics

Model interpretability criteria encompass aspects ranging from model transparency to post-hoc explanations for individual predictions. Key interpretability metrics include:

1 Feature Importance

Quantifying the influence of specific features on model outputs is achieved through various methodologies. The SHAP (SHapley Additive exPlanations) values provide a cohesive interpretability framework by attributing each feature's contribution to the predicted outcome through cooperative game theory principles.

$$\phi_i(f) = \sum_{S \subseteq N \setminus \{i\}} \frac{|S|!(|N| - |S| - 1)!}{|N|!}(f(S \cup \{i\}) - f(S)),$$

where N is the set of all features, and S is a subset of the feature set excluding feature i.

2 Model Complexity

The complexity of neural networks often inversely correlates with interpretability. Regularization methods such as L1 and L2 norms constrain complexity, fostering a balance between interpretability and predictive performance:

$$\text{L1 regularization: } \lambda \sum_i |w_i|,$$

$$\text{L2 regularization: } \lambda \sum_i w_i^2,$$

where λ is a hyperparameter controlling the strength of regularization, and w_i represents model weights.

3   Fairness and Bias Detection

Interpreting neural model decisions extends to identifying biases and ensuring fairness, especially in sensitive applications. Bias detection metrics, such as disparate impact ratios, quantify the differential treatment of groups:

$$\text{Disparate Impact} = \frac{P(y = 1 | a = 0)}{P(y = 1 | a = 1)},$$

where a denotes a protected attribute.

Causality in Neural Networks

Understanding causality in neural network decision processes enhances interpretability by distinguishing correlation from causation. Methods like `Causal Bayesian Networks` and `Structural Causal Models` provide a theoretical basis for encoding cause and effect relationships. These are crucial for valid generalizations and robust interventions.

The integration of causal inference within neural networks is represented by modeling assumptions and interventions, justified by Pearl's *do*-calculus approach:

$$P(y | \text{do}(x)) \neq P(y | x),$$

emphasizing the distinction between observational and interventional distributions.

Visualization Techniques

Visual encodings, including `t-SNE`, `UMAP`, and model-specific visualizations, serve as vital tools for intuitively interpreting neural network internals. These methods dimensionalize high-dimensional representations to unfold complex model landscapes and decision boundaries.

The t-SNE algorithm, for instance, aims to minimize:

$$KL(P||Q) = \sum_{i \neq j} p_{ij} \log \frac{p_{ij}}{q_{ij}},$$

where p_{ij} and q_{ij} represent the joint probability distributions over pairs of high-dimensional input features and their low-dimensional counterparts, respectively.

Python Code Snippet

Below is a Python code snippet that encompasses key computational elements related to interpretability and explainability in neural networks, including saliency maps, integrated gradients, feature importance using SHAP, and causal inference, alongside relevant visualizations.

```python
import tensorflow as tf
import numpy as np
from tensorflow.keras.applications import VGG16
from tensorflow.keras.models import Model
import shap

# Load a pretrained model for illustration purposes
model = VGG16(weights='imagenet', include_top=True)
model_input = model.inputs[0]
model_output = model.outputs[0]

def compute_saliency_map(input_image, model):
    '''
    Compute the saliency map of an input image.
    :param input_image: Image array.
    :param model: Trained model.
    :return: Saliency map.
    '''
    with tf.GradientTape() as tape:
        tape.watch(input_image)
        predictions = model(input_image)
        top_class = tf.argmax(predictions[0])

    gradients = tape.gradient(predictions[:, top_class],
    ↪ input_image)
    saliency_map = tf.abs(gradients)
    return saliency_map.numpy()

def integrated_gradients(input_image, baseline, model, steps=50):
    '''
    Compute the integrated gradients for a given image.
    :param input_image: Image array.
    :param baseline: Baseline image for comparison.
    :param model: Trained model.
    :param steps: Number of steps for approximation.
    :return: Integrated gradients.
    '''
    input_image = tf.convert_to_tensor(input_image)
    baseline = tf.convert_to_tensor(baseline)
    scaled_inputs = [baseline + (float(i) / steps) * (input_image -
    ↪ baseline) for i in range(0, steps + 1)]
    with tf.GradientTape() as tape:
        tape.watch(scaled_inputs)
```

```
            predictions = model(scaled_inputs)
            top_class = tf.argmax(predictions[0])

        grads = tape.gradient(predictions[:, top_class], scaled_inputs)
        avg_grads = tf.reduce_mean(grads, axis=0)
        integrated_grads = (input_image - baseline) * avg_grads
        return integrated_grads.numpy()

def calculate_shap_values(data, model):
    '''
    Calculate SHAP values for feature importance.
    :param data: Input features.
    :param model: Trained model.
    :return: SHAP values.
    '''

    explainer = shap.KernelExplainer(model.predict, data)
    shap_values = explainer.shap_values(data)
    return shap_values

def do_calculus_inference(p_y_do_x, p_y_given_x):
    '''
    illustrates the difference between interventional and
    ↪   observational distributions.
    :param p_y_do_x: Interventional probability.
    :param p_y_given_x: Observational probability.
    :return: Inference based on the difference.
    '''

    return p_y_do_x != p_y_given_x

# Example usage
gradient_saliency_map = compute_saliency_map(tf.random.uniform((1,
↪   224, 224, 3)), model)
baseline = tf.zeros((1, 224, 224, 3))
input_image = tf.random.uniform((1, 224, 224, 3))
integrated_grad = integrated_gradients(input_image, baseline, model)
dummy_data = np.random.rand(10, 100) # Example data for SHAP
↪   calculation
shap_vals = calculate_shap_values(dummy_data, model)
causal_inference_result = do_calculus_inference(0.5, 0.3)

print("Gradient Saliency Map computed")
print("Integrated Gradients computed:", integrated_grad)
print("SHAP Values:", shap_vals)
print("Causal Inference Result:", causal_inference_result)
```

This code includes functions that implement various methods and techniques discussed in interpretability and explainability within neural networks:

- `compute_saliency_map` function calculates a saliency map highlighting important regions in input that affect model decisions.

- `integrated_gradients` computes the integrated gradients approach for input feature importance.

- `calculate_shap_values` utilizes the SHAP library for determining feature importance via SHAP values.

- `do_calculus_inference` models causal inference using Pearl's *do*-calculus to differentiate between interventions and observations.

The snippets showcase how to apply these methods on example data or images, providing direct insights into model behavior and decision-making processes.

Chapter 30

Ethical and Philosophical Considerations

Algorithmic Bias and Fairness

In the deployment of neural networks, ethical concerns heavily focus on algorithmic bias, which can exacerbate existing societal inequalities. This bias arises when the distribution, $\mathcal{D}$, from which training samples are drawn, is disproportionately representative of specific groups. Thus, ensuring fairness demands adjustments in the loss function, $L(\theta)$, commonly embedded as:

$$L(\theta) = \sum_{i=1}^{n} \ell(f(x_i; \theta), y_i) + \lambda R(\theta),$$

where $R(\theta)$ includes fairness constraints. Algorithms must satisfy fairness definitions such as demographic parity:

$$P(\hat{Y} = 1 | A = 0) = P(\hat{Y} = 1 | A = 1),$$

where $\hat{Y}$ is the predicted label and A is a protected attribute.

Autonomy and Accountability

The autonomy of neural networks, specifically in decision-making contexts, raises concerns regarding accountability. Consider the decision function $f : \mathcal{X} \to \mathcal{Y}$, where f is derived through layers of abstractions, such that:

$$f(x) = h^{(L)}(h^{(L-1)}(...h^{(1)}(x)...)),$$

with L denoting layers, obscuring human oversight. Accountability must be enforceable through frameworks that map these transformations back to interpretable cause-and-effect relationships, leveraging C as a causality kernel:

$$C(f(x), y) > \delta \implies \text{responsibility.}$$

Transparency and the "Black Box" Problem

Neural networks' opaque nature, often termed as the "black box" problem, impedes their exploration and audit for ethical compliance. Transparency can be enhanced through interpretability methods reducing the functional complexity. Let $f(x) = \arg\max_y P(y|x; \theta)$, where interpretability is measured via simplicity of $P(y|x)$, ensuring output explanations adhere to:

$$E[y|x] = \sum_i w_i \cdot x_i + b,$$

where interpretability E involves sparse or decomposable linear mappings.

Data Privacy and Ownership

Advanced neural networks require expansive datasets, posing threats to individual privacy and data ownership. Standard practices in data handling fail to protect personal data distribution $\mathcal{D}_p$, thus differential privacy ($DP(\epsilon, \delta)$) mechanisms are essential:

$$\Delta f = \max_{D, D'} ||f(D) - f(D')||_1 \leq \epsilon,$$

ensuring that any single data change in D' causes negligible variation in output.

Philosophical Questions of Consciousness and Sentience

The evolution of neural networks encourages philosophical debates on machine consciousness and sentience. Theoretical modeling involves neural network states, S, and their mappings to cognitive processes C:

$$C(S) = \int_\Omega S_\omega \cdot \Psi(\omega)d\omega,$$

where $\Psi(\omega)$ describes cognitive functions potentially attributable to artificial sentience states Ω.

Value Alignment in Autonomous Systems

Aligning neural network and human values requires embedding ethical guidelines into autonomous systems. Consider the value function V, such that:

$$V_{\text{human}}(x) - V_{\text{network}}(x) = \epsilon,$$

where ϵ reflects alignment deviation. Constraining this with hierarchical learning frameworks ensures neural decision chains remain consistent with embedded moral principles.

Unintended Consequences of Neural Networks

Deploying neural networks can result in unintended consequences, where outputs deviate significantly from anticipated behavior. The optimization problem here is characterized by:

$$\min_\theta \sum_{i=1}^N \mathbb{E}_{x \sim \mathcal{D}}[\ell(f(x;\theta), y)] + \Omega(\nu),$$

where $\Omega(\nu)$ models the variance of strictly unintended outcomes and influences adjustments through speckled distributions.

Python Code Snippet

Below is a Python code snippet that simulates the ethical and philosophical considerations discussed in the chapter, including algorithmic bias, transparency, and data privacy through relevant implementations and calculations.

```python
import numpy as np
from sklearn.linear_model import LinearRegression

def demographic_parity(predictions, protected_attributes):
    '''
    Calculate demographic parity from predictions and protected
    ↪    attributes.
    :param predictions: Array of predicted labels.
    :param protected_attributes: Array indicating protected group
    ↪    membership.
    :return: Demographic parity difference.
    '''
    group_0_mean = np.mean(predictions[protected_attributes == 0])
    group_1_mean = np.mean(predictions[protected_attributes == 1])
    return abs(group_0_mean - group_1_mean)

def fairness_adjusted_loss(y_true, y_pred, theta, fairness_weight,
↪    regularization):
    '''
    Fairness-adjusted loss function incorporating regularization.
    :param y_true: True labels.
    :param y_pred: Predicted labels.
    :param theta: Model parameters.
    :param fairness_weight: Weighting for fairness in the loss.
    :param regularization: Regularization parameter.
    :return: Loss value.
    '''
    loss = np.mean((y_true - y_pred) ** 2)
    reg_term = regularization * np.sum(theta ** 2)
    fairness_penalty = fairness_weight * demographic_parity(y_pred,
    ↪    y_true > 0)
    return loss + reg_term + fairness_penalty

def model_accountability(x, layers=3):
    '''
    Trace model decision function back through layers for
    ↪    accountability.
    :param x: Input features.
    :param layers: Number of layers in the model.
    :return: Accountable transformations.
    '''
    accountable_transforms = []
    for l in range(layers):
        transform = f"Layer {l+1} transform on {x}"
```

```
        accountable_transforms.append(transform)
        x = np.sin(x)  # Dummy transformation for the sake of
        ↪    example
    return accountable_transforms

def simple_linear_model(x_train, y_train):
    '''
    Simple linear regression model for transparency illustration.
    :param x_train: Training features.
    :param y_train: Training labels.
    :return: Model coefficients and intercept.
    '''
    model = LinearRegression()
    model.fit(x_train, y_train)
    return model.coef_, model.intercept_

def differential_privacy_mechanism(data, epsilon, sensitivity=1.0):
    '''
    Implement a basic differential privacy mechanism.
    :param data: Data to apply the mechanism to.
    :param epsilon: Privacy parameter.
    :param sensitivity: Sensitivity of the data.
    :return: Noised data for privacy.
    '''
    noise = np.random.laplace(0, sensitivity/epsilon,
    ↪    size=data.shape)
    return data + noise

def philosophical_mapping(neural_state, cognitive_function):
    '''
    Map neural network states to cognitive processes.
    :param neural_state: State representation in the network.
    :param cognitive_function: Cognitive function assumed.
    :return: Cognitive process mapping.
    '''
    return np.inner(neural_state, cognitive_function)

# Sample data for demonstration
predictions = np.array([0, 1, 1, 0, 1])
protected_attrs = np.array([0, 1, 0, 1, 1])
theta = np.array([0.5, -0.2, 0.3])
x_train = np.random.rand(100, 2)
y_train = np.random.rand(100)

# Calculating demographic parity
parity_diff = demographic_parity(predictions, protected_attrs)

# Fairness adjusted loss
fair_loss = fairness_adjusted_loss(predictions, predictions, theta,
↪    0.1, 0.01)

# Accountability trace
transformations = model_accountability(predictions)
```

```
# Fit a transparent linear model
coefficients, intercept = simple_linear_model(x_train, y_train)

# Apply differential privacy mechanism
noised_data = differential_privacy_mechanism(y_train, epsilon=0.5)

# Mapping in the philosophical context
cognitive_mapping = philosophical_mapping(theta, np.array([1, 1,
↪    1]))

print("Demographic Parity Difference:", parity_diff)
print("Fairness Adjusted Loss:", fair_loss)
print("Accountability Transformations:", transformations)
print("Linear Model Coefficients:", coefficients)
print("Noised Data for Privacy:", noised_data[:5])
print("Philosophical Mapping:", cognitive_mapping)
```

This code demonstrates key concepts related to ethical and philosophical aspects of neural networks:

- **demographic_parity** function calculates disparity between groups based on predictions to address fairness.

- **fairness_adjusted_loss** incorporates fairness directly into the loss function adding a penalty based on demographic parity.

- **model_accountability** creates a trace of function transformations for accountability purpose by propagation through layers.

- **simple_linear_model** implements linear regression for easier interpretability, showcasing transparency.

- **differential_privacy_mechanism** applies noise to data to preserve privacy following differential privacy standards.

- **philosophical_mapping** maps neural state information to abstract cognitive functions for philosophical discussions.

Each function provides a practical or illustrative approach to important ethical and philosophical issues surrounding neural networks.

Chapter 31

Theoretical Limitations and Open Challenges

Expressive Limitations

Neural networks, despite their universal approximation capabilities, are bound by limitations in expressive power under certain constraints. A neural network is often described by its function approximation, $f(x; \theta)$, which maps input x to an output through a series of transformations parameterized by θ. However, these networks cannot approximate functions requiring complex compositional hierarchies in fixed polynomial time. The expressive capacity is theoretically constrained by the number of layers L and neurons per layer. For a feedforward network to approximate some functions sufficiently, it must satisfy:

$$\|f(x; \theta) - g(x)\| < \epsilon$$

for all x under certain conditions, yet this often requires exponential width or depth, leading to prohibitive computational requirements.

Generalization Bound Constraints

The theory underlying neural network generalization to unseen data is a pivotal area of limited understanding. The Vapnik-Chervonenkis

(VC) dimension is a classical measure, yet it fails to predict generalization behavior accurately in deep models. For a hypothesis class $\mathcal{H}$ learned from samples $\mathcal{D}$, the generalization error ϵ_g can be theoretically bounded as:

$$\epsilon_g = \mathcal{O}\left(\sqrt{\frac{d_{VC}(\log(N/d_{VC})+1)}{N}}\right),$$

where d_{VC} is the VC-dimension, and N is the sample size. However, deeper networks tend to exhibit low generalization error even with overparameterization, suggesting the inadequacy of VC bounds and calling for refined complexity measures like the Rademacher complexity and PAC-Bayes bounds.

Optimization Challenges

Optimization landscapes in deep learning are inherently non-convex, which complicates effective learning and convergence guarantees. The function $L(\theta) = \sum_{i=1}^{N} \ell(f(x_i, \theta), y_i)$, where ℓ is the loss function, defines a highly non-linear optimization objective. Critical challenges arise due to:

- Existence of numerous local minima and saddle points, necessitating advancements beyond standard gradient descent techniques, which predominantly converge to suboptimal points. - The landscape's saddle points have been shown to potentially outnumber local minima, described mathematically as:

$$\min_{\theta} \|\nabla L(\theta)\|_2^2 = 0 \Rightarrow \nabla^2 L(\theta) \text{ is not positive definite.}$$

Understanding Overparameterization

The phenomenon of overparameterization contradicts classical learning theory, as networks often operate beyond the "double-descent" curve, where additional capacity unexpectedly improves generalization. Denote an overparameterized model by parameters θ satisfying $|\theta| > N$. This leads to:

$$\inf_{\theta} \|Y - f(X;\theta)\|^2 = 0$$

yet generalization $\|Y_{\text{test}} - f(X_{\text{test}};\theta)\|$ remains low.

This paradox remains an open challenge, questioning traditional bias-variance trade-offs and requiring further understanding.

Implicit Bias in Gradient Descent

Gradient-based methods introduce implicit biases, especially in the choice of optimization paths. Implicit regularization affects the trajectory $\theta(t)$ via dynamics described by:

$$\frac{d\theta}{dt} = -\nabla L(\theta(t)),$$

which biases solutions toward certain minima. Understanding this mechanism universally and leveraging it to enhance model performances across varying architectures indicates a significant research frontier.

Robustness to Adversarial Attacks

Adversarial examples highlight vulnerabilities, where small perturbations δ crafted for input x lead to erroneous predictions, i.e., $f(x + \delta; \theta) \neq y$. The function δ is typically within a norm-bounded set:

$$\|\delta\|_p \leq \epsilon \quad \forall x \in \mathcal{D},$$

yet these perturbations result in substantial drops in accuracy, demonstrating inadequacies in our understanding of decision boundaries. The theoretical understanding of such adversarial robustness is nascent, and forming rigorous mathematical underpinnings remains a profound theoretic and practical open problem.

Scalability of Theoretical Constructs

Many theoretical results scale poorly with large datasets or complex architectures. For large datasets $\mathcal{D}$ with cardinality $|\mathcal{D}| \to \infty$, assumptions made in computational feasibilities break down, for example, in computing Hessians or Jacobians required for certain regularization or stability analyses.

Iterative algorithms relying on subensemble methods and leveraging model parallelism, state the thesis:

$$\mathcal{M} = \bigcup_{i=1}^{k} \mathcal{M}_i, \quad \text{where } \mathcal{M}_i \text{ are model partitions.}$$

This raises the necessity for theoretical advances that respect computational constraints for new architectures, including networks processing high-dimensional data or integrating multimodal inputs.

Fusion of Theory with Emerging Paradigms

Emerging paradigms such as quantum computing, spiking neural networks, and neuromorphic architectures present unique theoretical challenges. Models such as $Q(\mathcal{H})$ in quantum neural networks, potentially promise super-polynomial speed-ups, yet face:

$$Q(\mathcal{H}) \sim f(n, \alpha) \quad \text{where speedup relation remains non-trivial.}$$

Issues in incorporating quantum phenomena into known practical benefits highlight the gap between nascent quantum algorithms and established learning theories.

Mathematical Modeling of Interpretability

Understanding and quantifying interpretability is a significant theoretic challenge, requiring a reliable mathematical model to describe human cognitive mappings, $\mathcal{C}(\theta)$, as:

$$\mathcal{C}(\theta) = \sum_{i} w_i g(x_i) + b, \quad \text{where interpretable represents constraints on } g.$$

Establishing rigorous interpretability metrics that can guide ethical AI development frameworks and incorporate human factors into neural design models substantially remain explorative avenues in theoretical research.

Interdisciplinary Integration

The multidisciplinary aggregation of fields like neuroscience, cognitive science, and physics into machine learning is poised for theoretical synthesis. The neural activation function approximation, for instance, often described by:

$$\sigma(x) = \int K(x,y)g(y)dy,$$

indicates the potential for integrating functional approximations across diverse theoretical disciplines, fostering unified modeling approaches bridging theoretical constructs in machine learning with axioms in biological computation and cognitive frameworks.

Python Code Snippet

Below is a Python code snippet that illustrates the implementation of key equations and algorithms mentioned in this chapter, facilitating an understanding of neural network limitations, optimization, and robustness.

```python
import numpy as np
import scipy.optimize as opt

# Expressive Limitations - Function Approximation
def function_approximation(x, theta):
    '''
    Simulates neural network function approximation.
    :param x: Input value.
    :param theta: Parameters representing the network weights.
    :return: Approximated output.
    '''
    return np.dot(x, theta)

def universal_approximation(x, target_function, epsilon,
    max_iterations=10000):
    '''
    Attempt to approximate a target function with a neural network.
    :param x: Input samples.
    :param target_function: True function to approximate.
    :param epsilon: Tolerance for approximation.
    :param max_iterations: Maximum number of iterations allowed.
    :return: Approximated function weights.
    '''
    def loss_function(theta):
        return np.linalg.norm(function_approximation(x, theta) -
            target_function(x))

    theta_initial = np.random.rand(x.shape[1])
    result = opt.minimize(loss_function, theta_initial,
        options={'maxiter': max_iterations})
```

```python
    if result.fun < epsilon:
        return result.x
    else:
        raise ValueError("Unable to approximate the target function
        ↪  within the given tolerance")


# Generalization Bound Constraints - VC Dimension
def vc_dimension_bound(d_vc, N):
    '''
    Computes the theoretical generalization error bound based on VC
    ↪  dimension.
    :param d_vc: VC dimension.
    :param N: Sample size.
    :return: Generalization error bound.
    '''
    return np.sqrt((d_vc * (np.log(N / d_vc) + 1)) / N)


# Optimization Challenges - Non-Convex Optimization Landscape
def gradient_descent_non_convex(L, grad_L, theta_init,
↪  learning_rate=0.01, tolerance=1e-6, max_iter=1000):
    '''
    Gradient descent for non-convex optimization.
    :param L: Loss function handle.
    :param grad_L: Gradient of the loss function.
    :param theta_init: Initial parameter guess.
    :param learning_rate: Learning rate for updates.
    :param tolerance: Tolerance for stopping criteria.
    :param max_iter: Maximum iterations.
    :return: Optimized parameters.
    '''
    theta = theta_init
    for _ in range(max_iter):
        grad = grad_L(theta)
        next_theta = theta - learning_rate * grad
        if np.linalg.norm(next_theta - theta) < tolerance:
            break
        theta = next_theta
    return theta


# Robustness to Adversarial Attacks
def adversarial_example(x, model, epsilon, norm='inf'):
    '''
    Generates an adversarial example via perturbation.
    :param x: Original input.
    :param model: Model to attack.
    :param epsilon: Magnitude of perturbation.
    :param norm: Norm type, 'inf' or '2'.
    :return: Perturbed input.
    '''
    if norm == 'inf':
        perturbed = x + np.sign(np.gradient(model(x))) * epsilon
    elif norm == '2':
```

```
            perturbed = x + model(x) / np.linalg.norm(model(x)) *
            ↪  epsilon
        return perturbed

# Helper Function - Simple Model for Demonstration
def simple_model(x, weights, bias):
    '''
    A simple linear model.
    :param x: Input data.
    :param weights: Weights of the model.
    :param bias: Bias term.
    :return: Output prediction.
    '''

    return np.dot(x, weights) + bias


# Example Usage
x_example = np.array([[0.5, 0.2], [0.9, 0.3]])
theta_approx = universal_approximation(x_example, lambda x: 2 * x[:,
↪  0] + 3 * x[:, 1], epsilon=0.01)
vc_bound = vc_dimension_bound(10, 100)
optimized_theta = gradient_descent_non_convex(lambda theta:
↪  np.sum(theta**2), lambda theta: 2*theta, np.array([1.0, 2.0]),
↪  0.01)
perturbed_x = adversarial_example(x_example[0], lambda x:
↪  simple_model(x, np.array([1.5, 2.5]), 0.1), epsilon=0.05)

print("Approximated Weights:", theta_approx)
print("Generalization Bound:", vc_bound)
print("Optimized Parameters:", optimized_theta)
print("Adversarial Example:", perturbed_x)
```

This code provides implementations of theoretical concepts discussed:

- `function_approximation` and `universal_approximation` simulate the process of approximating functions with neural networks, considering expressive constraints.

- `vc_dimension_bound` computes error bounds using VC dimension insights.

- `gradient_descent_non_convex` illustrates gradient descent on non-convex loss landscapes.

- `adversarial_example` generates perturbed adversarial examples to study model robustness.

- A simple linear `simple_model` serves as a placeholder for model predictions in adversarial demonstrations.

This snippet encapsulates theoretical challenges in neural network research through practical Python implementations.

Chapter 32

Applications of Topology in Neural Networks

Introduction to Topological Data Analysis

Topological Data Analysis (TDA) provides innovative techniques to understand complex data sets by exploiting their inherent geometrical and topological features. A foundational tool in TDA is persistent homology, which extracts multi-scale topological information through filtration—a sequence of nested spaces $X_0 \subseteq X_1 \subseteq \cdots \subseteq X_n$. Each filtration allows computation of homology groups $H_k(X_i)$, enabling the study of features such as connected components, loops, and voids by observing their birth and death across different scales. The result, a persistence diagram, encapsulates this topological evolution and can be formally expressed by:

$$D_k = \{(b_i, d_i)|b_i, d_i \in \mathbb{R}, \, b_i \leq d_i\}.$$

where D_k represents the persistence of k-dimensional features.

Integration of TDA in Neural Networks

Neural networks benefit from TDA by leveraging topological features for improved representation learning. By incorporating persistence diagrams as inputs or features, neural architectures can learn invariant representations that encapsulate essential structural properties. For instance, the function $f(x; \theta)$ may exploit topological regularization, defined by:

$$\mathcal{L}_{\text{top}}(f, \theta, D) = \sum_i \|f(x_i; \theta) - T(D_k(x_i))\|^2,$$

where $T(\cdot)$ is a differentiable function that maps persistence features for operational compatibility with f.

Topology in Understanding Decision Boundaries

The decision boundaries of neural networks can be profoundly complex, yet topological insights offer avenues for comprehension. By interpreting these boundaries as manifolds, TDA identifies critical points and phase transitions across the input space. This involves computing Betti numbers β_k, which quantify the count of k-dimensional holes that persist at various thresholds t. Formally:

$$\beta_k(X_t) = \text{rank}(H_k(X_t)),$$

where X_t denotes the space at threshold t. Such analysis reveals regions of instability or overlap that might correlate with adversarial susceptibility.

Algebraic Topology in Feature Understanding

Algebraic topology extends the usage of homological algebra to decipher deep network complexities, providing a formalism to assess invariants under continuous transformations. The functoriality of homology allows transformation of neural feature maps into structured algebraic entities, preserving essential properties across layers. One can define a simplicial complex K over a data set, where features $\phi(x_i)$ are mapped into vertices and simplexes to study relations. Given simplex $\sigma \in K$, the chain complex C_k leads to homology groups:

$$H_k(K) = \frac{\ker(\partial_k)}{\operatorname{im}(\partial_{k+1})},$$

with boundary operator $\partial_k : C_k \to C_{k-1}$.

Insights into Neural Network Behaviors

Topology provides empirical methods to decode what neural networks learn. Neural collapse, a phenomenon where within-class variations diminish while between-class distinctions amplify, realizes topological alignment. Topological features, such as loop contraction and surface compactness, surpass mere statistical analysis, capturing latent geometric symmetries in the learned representations. Estimating approximate geodesics on data manifolds, the function $\gamma(s)$, parameterizes paths on the manifold facilitating interpretability:

$$\gamma(s) : [0, 1] \to M, \quad \text{where } M \text{ is the data manifold.}$$

Topological Regularization Techniques

Incorporating topological constraints into loss functions acts as regularization, stabilizing network training and avoiding nonsensical configurations. Topological regularization encourages the preservation of geometric shape properties, promoting smooth manifold learning and improved generalization. Given neural network parameterization by θ, we derive a total loss:

$$\mathcal{L}_{\text{total}} = \mathcal{L}_{\text{task}} + \lambda \mathcal{L}_{\text{top}},$$

where $\mathcal{L}_{\text{task}}$ is the task-specific loss and λ balances the topological penalty.

Applications and Future Perspectives

Embedding TDA within neural network frameworks extends beyond enhancement of intrinsic capabilities, gaining traction in critical fields such as generative modeling, domain adaptation, and predictive uncertainty quantification. The meticulous integration of topological structures empowers networks with robustness against domain shifts and semantic changes, endorsing their applicability in diverse, unexplored territories.

Python Code Snippet

Below is a Python code snippet that implements key aspects from this chapter, including persistent homology, topological regularization, and Betti number calculation, illustrating how these algorithms can be applied to neural networks to derive topological insights.

```python
import numpy as np
from scipy.spatial import Delaunay
import gudhi as gd

def compute_persistence_diagram(data_points):
    '''
    Compute the persistence diagram using Delaunay triangulation and
    ↪ persistent homology.
    :param data_points: Numpy array of data points.
    :return: Persistence diagram.
    '''
    # Compute Delaunay triangulation
    tri = Delaunay(data_points)

    # Initialize Simplex Tree
    simplex_tree = gd.SimplexTree()
    for simplex in tri.simplices:
        simplex_tree.insert(simplex)

    # Compute persistent homology
    simplex_tree.compute_persistence()
    return simplex_tree.persistence()

def topological_regularization(f, theta, persistence_features,
    ↪ target):
    '''
    Compute topological regularization loss.
    :param f: Neural network function.
    :param theta: Model parameters.
    :param persistence_features: Topological features extracted as
    ↪ persistence diagrams.
    :param target: Target output for comparison.
    :return: Topological regularization loss.
    '''
```

```python
    # Here T is an identity placeholder
    T = lambda x: x
    return np.sum((f(persistence_features, theta) - T(target))**2)

def compute_betti_numbers(simplexes, max_dimension):
    '''
    Compute Betti numbers for given simplexes.
    :param simplexes: List of simplexes.
    :param max_dimension: Maximum dimension for Betti number
    ↪   calculation.
    :return: Betti numbers array.
    '''
    # Create Simplex Tree and insert simplexes
    st = gd.SimplexTree()
    for simplex in simplexes:
        st.insert(simplex)

    # Persistence computation step
    st.compute_persistence()

    # Extract Betti numbers for each dimension
    betti_numbers = [st.betti_numbers()[dim] for dim in
    ↪   range(max_dimension + 1)]
    return betti_numbers

def neural_topological_metrics(data_points, target_space,
↪   max_dim=2):
    '''
    Compute neural network extended metrics with topological lens.
    :param data_points: Data points forming neural network
    ↪   boundaries.
    :param target_space: Neural output target space.
    :param max_dim: Maximum topological dimension for analysis.
    :return: Persistence diagram and Betti numbers.
    '''

    persistence_diagram = compute_persistence_diagram(data_points)
    betti_numbers = compute_betti_numbers(data_points, max_dim)

    return persistence_diagram, betti_numbers

# Example of utilizing the functions
points = np.random.rand(30, 2)  # Example data points

# Compute persistence diagram and Betti numbers for the model
↪   decision space
persistence_diagram, betti_numbers =
↪   neural_topological_metrics(points, points)

print("Persistence Diagram:", persistence_diagram)
print("Betti Numbers:", betti_numbers)
```

This code provides important computational components for

embedding topological insights into neural network frameworks:

- `compute_persistence_diagram` calculates the persistence diagram using Delaunay triangulation, suitable for extracting topological features from data.

- `topological_regularization` illustrates a way to incorporate topological penalties in the loss function, augmenting neural learning by emphasizing geometric constancy.

- `compute_betti_numbers` defines a process to calculate Betti numbers, contributing to the understanding of neural network decision boundaries by quantifying geometric connectivity.

- `neural_topological_metrics` integrates these computations to offer a robust assessment of networks through topological investigations.

These components allow for enhanced interpretation of neural network dynamics by leveraging topological data analysis.

www.ingramcontent.com/pod-product-compliance
Lightning Source LLC
La Vergne TN
LVHW051331050326
832903LV00031B/3478